A CATHOLIC VOTE FOR TRUMP

A

CATHOLIC
VOTE

FOR

TRUMP

The Only Choice in 2020 for
Republicans, Democrats, and
Independents Alike

JESSE ROMERO
WITH JOHN MCCULLOUGH

TAN Books
Gastonia, North Carolina

Unless otherwise noted, Scripture quotations are from the Revised Standard Version of the Bible—Second Catholic Edition (Ignatius Edition), copyright © 2006 National Council of the Churches of Christ in the United States of America. Used by permission. All rights reserved.

Excerpts from the English translation of the Catechism of the Catholic Church for use in the United States of America copyright © 1994, United States Catholic Conference, Inc.—Libreria Editrice Vaticana. Used with permission.

Passages from papal documents, encyclicals, and addresses © Libreria Editrice Vaticana unless otherwise noted. All rights reserved. Used with permission.

Excerpts from James Howard Kunstler's blog © James Howard Kustler. All rights reserved. Used by permission of the Author.

Brian Cates article © Brian Cates 2020 and UncoverDC.com. Used by permission of Author and Publisher.

Excerpts from *The Last Refuge* www.theconservativetreehouse.com. Used by permission.

List of Trump accomplishments in appendix 2 compiled by Robby Starbuck. Used by permission.

Cover image: US President Donald Trump walks to Marine One on the South Lawn of the White House December 21, 2017 in Washington, DC. / AFP PHOTO / Brendan Smialowski via Getty Images.

Closeup of American flag by STILLFX via Shutterstock

Library of Congress Control Number: 2020934235

Hardcover ISBN: 978-1-5051-1732-5
Paperback ISBN: 978-1-5051-1729-5

Published in the United States by
TAN Books
P.O. Box 269
Gastonia, NC 28053
www.TANBooks.com

Printed in the United States of America

To Melania and the Trump family, in gratitude for the sacrifices you have made and any suffering you may have endured so that your husband and father (and grandfather) can carry out the heroic task with which he has been entrusted.

JR and JM

To all my Latino Catholic brothers and sisters who have been deceived by the modernist liberal mainstream propagandist media. I hope this information helps the scales to fall from your eyes (cf. Acts 9:18).

JR

And with gratitude to two American heroes whose stories will be truthfully told one day, Lieutenant General Michael Flynn and Admiral Michael Rogers.

JM

Saint Michael the Archangel, defend us in battle. Be our protection against the wickedness and snares of the Devil. May God rebuke him we humbly pray, and do thou O Prince of the Heavenly Host, by the power of God, cast into Hell Satan and all evil spirits who prowl throughout the world seeking the ruin of souls. Amen.

No one can be, at the same time, a sincere
Catholic and a true Socialist.

Pius XI, *Quadragesimo Anno*, 1931

CONTENTS

FOREWORD

WHEN I do my daily broadcasts from our TV studio at our Priests for Life headquarters, I have a photo of President Donald Trump clearly visible behind me.

On a regular basis, one or another viewer, whose comments I can see during the broadcast, will ask, "Why do you have a picture of President Trump over your shoulder?"

I respond first by saying, "Well, this program is coming to you from the United States of America, and he is our president.

"And second, *if he were not where he is, we would not be where we are.*"

I pause for a moment to let that sink in, and then I explain further that under the Obama administration, Priests for Life was one of the religious groups that had to fight all the way to the Supreme Court to avoid crippling fines for our refusal to include abortion in the health insurance plan that we offer our employees.

The Supreme Court, in the end, didn't technically decide the case. Donald Trump did. The court had asked that we work out a solution with the administration, and the Obama administration was simply unwilling to honor our religious objections.

President Trump did, and we were forever set free from the oppressive mandate that, had it been enforced under a

President Hillary Clinton, would not have allowed our ministry—and countless others—to function.

If President Trump were not where he is, we would not be where we are.

Many voters, whose faith means something to them, realize this, and it's time that the rest did as well. That's why this book is so important and so timely.

Because religious people care about virtue, some will complain if they do not think the president is living out the Christian faith.

Now I reject the premise. I believe he does live the Christian faith. He is a man who believes in Christ, keeps his promises, protects his nation as his constitutional duties require him to do, loves his family and raises beautiful children ("By their fruits you will know them"), and is generous—including with his salary. A pastor who ministers to him said that he had rarely met a man more open to the Holy Spirit than President Trump.

He lives his faith.

But to those who think he doesn't, I ask, *would you rather have a president who does not live out his faith, or a president who does not allow you to live out your faith?*

No president has protected religious freedom and conscience more than President Trump. And he has done so proactively, putting in place executive policies that enable faith-based organizations to do their work with fewer obstacles, and without discrimination, and punishing institutions that violate existing law that protects religious freedom. President Trump even created a new federal office to protect conscience and religious freedom!

There's another dimension to consider as well. This election is not about personalities. It is about a clash of worldviews, which shape multiple issues, far beyond the most fundamental ones of abortion and religious freedom.

The election is not about *private* virtue; it is about *public* virtue. Instead of worrying about the president's marriages, ask yourself what impact the judges he appoints will make on the shape of marriage in our country for the next generation. Instead of worrying how religious he is, ask yourself what impact his policies will have on the Church's freedom to help people live out their religion for the next generation. Instead of being concerned about the tweets he sends, pay more attention to the laws he signs. It's the *public virtue,* not the private virtue, that should shape our vote.

Pro-abortion Democrats try to make us focus on what they *believe in private* about abortion, as an excuse for us to ignore *the public policies they create* that make it continue. Let's not make the same mistake in reverse.

The president himself has said that the election is not about him; it's about *you.* The attacks launched against him are really *attacks on you.* They are an attempt to deprive *you* of the impact of your vote and of your values on our public life. President Trump is just the messenger, the vehicle, of a whole set of policies and worldviews. Stay focused, ask the right questions, and see the big picture.

And think for yourself. Remember, Catholicism values human reason very highly and expects us to use it. You alone are responsible for your vote: not your parents and grandparents, not your union or your employer, and not even your pastor or bishop.

Elections are not just about putting a person into office; that person brings with him or her a whole philosophy and a vast network of appointed officials to carry it out.

In the elections of 2020, we are not simply asked to choose between Donald Trump and his opponent.

We are being asked to choose either

- the culture of life or the culture of death,
- religious freedom or religious oppression,
- prosperity or poverty,
- a secure nation or open borders,
- patriotism or globalism,
- a free market or socialism,
- the Constitution or judicial tyranny,
- law and order or anarchy,
- and much more.

This book helps to outline the choice, and I am grateful to its authors.

We at Priests for Life will also help you to act upon what you learn in this book. At ProLifeVote.com, we have an entire operation in place to help you make a difference in these elections. Please visit there and get involved today.

There has never been a more consequential election in our history; the options have never been more diametrically opposed, and the choice has never been clearer.

Let's keep America great!

Fr. Frank Pavone, National Director, Priests for Life

PREFACE

"Papa, how can you vote for him?" my then thirteen-year-old son asked me one night in 2016. "He's so crude." The "him" of the question was, of course, then candidate Donald John Trump. I answered:

> Brendan, I know he swears and is crude, but so are a lot of the best men I've ever known. I've known guys who talk like sailors and haven't darkened the door of a church in years, if not decades. And they would give you the shirt off their back.[1] And I've known men who present themselves as holier than thou and would certainly never use bad words, but they'd stab you in the back and not think twice about it. Trump is crude, but those other men so worried about what he says have had their chance to run the country. A lot of those men (and women) in those debates and other pundits who express outrage at Trump's coarseness have the ethnic cleansing and blood of hundreds of thousands of Christians on their hands from the Middle East wars that unleashed hell on those poor people. That's crude. And they're worried about swearing and rough

---

[1] This observation does not minimize the grave obligation these good men have, if Catholic, to return to the sacraments and the practice of the faith of their fathers. As a priest friend of mine is fond of saying, "Eternity is a long time."

language? Have those Catholics who judge Trump but supported those disastrous policies apologized? He should be mad. He should be swearing. Drive around the country and look at what has been done (not happened . . . what has been done) to the working class in this country while those guys make speeches and promises, and nothing ever changes for the better.

That was the way one Catholic father explained his support for Donald Trump when his son asked him. And his enthusiasm for the man did not wane. Later, when Hillary Clinton ran what was probably her most memorable television ad spot, the one which featured little kids transfixed in front of the TV screen while Trump seemingly shouted, "They can go f**k themselves,"[2] my son looked at me expectantly with a look that said, "What about that?" I replied, "That right there is why I'm voting for him."[3]

And, you know, it turns out I was not alone.

If you want to understand why Trump is the forty-fifth president, none other than Michael Moore, the ultra-liberal, Trump-hating filmmaker, told the world before the election why the man he hated was going to win. Watch the video found at the following URL: https://www.youtube.com/

---

[2]   He did, in fact, say it at a speech in New Hampshire in reference to companies leaving the United States, but he actually mouthed or whispered the f-word rather than shouted it.

[3]   It should go without saying that I was not telling my son that the mere fact of Trump's using coarse language was my reason for supporting the man; rather, I was telling him, and I explained this in greater detail at the time, that I supported the righteous indignation that lay behind the language, but truth be told, the language did not bother me.

watch?v=FLfvXjKMwtI. Don't feel bad if you are almost moved to tears. You should be. (If that URL is no longer active, search for Michael Moore Trump speech.)

Moore got it; in fact, he got it so well that one wonders why he did not support Trump. Well, not really, but that was as powerful a stump speech for Donald Trump in 2016 as you'll find. Moore's speech in Ohio to what looked like a crowd of rust belt Democrats, and hence, probably a lot of blue-collar Catholics, explained and justified, even if unintentionally,[4] the natural appeal of candidate Trump to such voters.

In that video, Moore is talking specifically about the economic destruction of the working class that has proceeded apace under politicians of both parties for the past four decades, if not longer, but he could just as well have talked about the wars to which the poor and middle class have sent their sons and daughters and for which the results have been nothing short of disastrous, especially, again, for the Christians in the Middle East. We couldn't have done a better job of making the world safe for radical Islam had we tried, that is, until Donald J. Trump was elected, and now, more than three years later, ISIS's territory has been rolled back. And our political leadership in Washington is unafraid to identify that particular enemy by name.

Many Catholics have wrestled with the candidacy and now the presidency of Donald Trump, often for very different reasons for he eludes easy categorization. Many of those

---

[4]   To be sure, the rest of Moore's speech could hardly be expected to support Trump, but those few minutes sure made a decent case, even if, perhaps especially if, unintentional.

who originally did not like him have warmed to him, again, for a variety of reasons. But one can assume that there are still many Catholics out there that either don't know what to make of the man or dislike him. As reflected in the subtitle of this book, the authors feel certain that for Catholics voting in the 2020 election, Trump is the only choice for Republicans, Democrats, and Independents alike. In these pages, we will endeavor to explain why.

How to Read This Book

A Catholic Vote for Trump endeavors to look at this man— one of the most polarizing figures in the history of American politics, yet at the same time one of the great unifiers, as he is drawing in Democrats and Independents of all races—and make the case that for Catholics, a vote for Trump is the only choice in 2020. To do so completely objectively is a daunting task, and the authors will claim to be fair-minded, but maybe not objective, for they have come to love Donald Trump. In the draft stage, the working subtitle of the book was "The Establishment Has No Clothes." That working subtitle captures the feeling of perhaps much of the country. What Trump revealed—and everyone knows that no one else would have revealed it either because they were, or still are, part of the whole corrupt enterprise, or because they did not believe it themselves, or because they simply would not have been able to pull back the curtain as masterfully as Trump has—is that, truly, the establishment has no clothes.

Trump was like the child in that story who told the truth, out loud, while everyone around him, lemming-like, admired the naked king's "clothes."

- On foolish wars and nation building, Trump said, "They have no clothes. No more stupid wars."
- On the trade deals that have gutted this country, Trump said, "They have no clothes. Let's bring back manufacturing and make America great again!"
- On the corruption and, as is being revealed, criminality endemic to DC, Trump said, "They have no clothes. Lock her up." (Recent events have revealed that the "her" of his rhetoric could well be changed to "them.")
- On the unchecked flow of immigrants over the southern border, Trump said, "They have no clothes. Illegal immigration today has nothing to do with the fact that the United States is a 'nation of immigrants.' The circumstances have changed. What do you do when the circumstances change? You change."
- On the corrupt and dishonest media, Trump said, "They have no clothes. Fake news!"
- On Islam as the religion of peace, Trump said, "They have no clothes. Radical Islamic Terrorism."
- On the fact that the political class in this country is essentially a uniparty and has not put the average American first, Trump said, "They have no clothes. Drain the Swamp."
- On the tragedy of abortion in this country, Trump said, "They have no clothes. I will be a pro-life president."[5]

---

[5] Lest we be accused of putting words into the President's mouth à la Adam Schiff, know that we are simply saying that these examples are what Trump, in essence, has said.

So, this book will look at Trump from a Catholic perspective touching upon a variety of themes and issues. Relevant quotes from Church teaching or other Catholic sources will introduce the chapters followed by pertinent quotes from Trump's speeches. In addition, the outstanding work of other commentators—from the Left, Right, and who knows where—will be quoted, at times at length, if they are particularly astute observers of what has gone on these past few years. Jesse will bring his particular perspective as a Mexican-American Catholic to bear on issues such as immigration. By drawing on a diversity of sources, it is hoped that this book will be viewed as something other than the special pleading of a particular political outlook, though the authors are staunch Catholics who come from long lines of Democrats, but who fairly early on in their own voting lives realized they could no longer stand with that party. As the years have passed, they have noticed more and more of their friends and family make that same break. URLs—some in the main body of the book itself but most in the footnotes—will be provided to important videos to watch and articles to read online that will be discussed in the text. If you find that the URLs are not current (though they are when the book goes to press), key words will also be provided to assist in the search. But one need not follow the links or read the other articles to understand the book.

JM

INTRODUCTION

Nothing can do men of good will more harm than apparent compromises with parties that subscribe to antimoral and antidemocratic and anti-God forces. We must have the courage to detach our support from men who are doing evil. We must bear them no hatred, but we must break with them.[1]

Fulton J. Sheen

*But wait a minute, wait a minute.
But the Catholic Church is pro-life.*[2]

Donald Trump to pro-choice Catholic Democrat Chris Matthews, March 2016

The Catholic Voter

THERE have been numerous sociological studies on the changing Catholic voter. Throughout much of the twentieth century, Catholics naturally gravitated towards the Democratic Party, and if you grew up Catholic in Boston or in the barrios of Los Angeles in the '50s, '60s, and '70s, you

---

[1]   Fulton J. Sheen, *Communism and the Conscience of the West* (New York: Bobbs-Merrill Company, 1948), p. 126.

[2]   Tom Kertscher, "In Context: Transcript of Donald Trump on punishing women for abortion," *Politifact*, March 30, 2016, https://www.politifact.com/article/2016/mar/30/context-trans cript-donald-trump-punishing-women-ab/.

probably socialized with even fewer Republicans than you did Protestants. But that has changed as the Democratic Party has tacked hard left and beyond, such that it seems if you are pro-life or anti-gay marriage or anti-drag queen story hours, your chances of finding a home at the national level in Democratic politics reside somewhere between slim and none on the probability scale, and slim has left the building.

Witness the January exchange between Kristen Day, the president of Democrats for Life, and Mayor Pete Buttigieg:

> KRISTEN DAY, AUDIENCE: I am a proud pro-life Democrat. So, do you want the support of pro-life Democrats, pro-life Democratic voters? There are about 21 million of us. And if so, would you support more moderate platform language in the Democratic Party to ensure that the party of diversity, of inclusion really does include everybody?
>
> BUTTIGIEG: . . . And the best that I can offer -- and it may win your vote and, if not, I understand -- the best I can offer is that if we can't agree on where to draw the line, the next best thing we can do is agree on who should draw the line. And in my view, it's the woman who's faced with that decision in her own life.

Asked by moderator Chris Wallace if she was satisfied with that answer, Day replied:

> No, I was not, because he did not answer the second part of my question. And the second part was, the Democratic platform contains language that basically says that we don't belong, we have no part in the party,

because it says abortion should be legal up to nine months, the government should pay for it, and there's nothing that says that people [who] have a diversity of views on this issue should be included in the party.

In 1996, and I guess several years after that, there was language in the Democratic platform that said that we understand that people have very differing views on this issue, but we are a big tent party that includes everybody. And so, therefore, we welcome you, people like me, into the party so we can work on issues that we agree on.

So my question was, would you be open to language like that in the Democratic platform, that really did say that our party is diverse and inclusive and we want everybody?[3]

Mayor Pete explained his support for the platform as written and concluded by saying, truthfully it must be said, which is to his credit: "And again, the best I can offer is that we may disagree on that very important issue, and hopefully we will be able to partner on other issues."

To which Day replied, cutting to the chase, "So that would be a no?"

Wallace concluded the exchange by noting, "I think it's fair to say Kristen is not clapping, but that's part of the process." Yes, it is part of the process, a process that has been

---

3   Ian Schwartz, "Pro-Life Democrat Grills Buttigieg At FOX News Town Hall: Party Platform Says We Don't Belong," *RealClear Politics*, January 26, 2020, https://www.realclearpolitics.com/video/2020/01/26/pro-life_democrat_grills_buttigieg_at_fox_news_town_hall_party_platform_says_we_dont_belong.html.

unfolding since *Roe v. Wade* was made the law of the land by judicial fiat, and one which may be approaching its denouement in terms of the relationship between Catholics and the Democratic Party. And when that relationship ends, the Democratic Party, for all intents and purposes, ends. To say nothing of when the Bernie Bros revolt if their candidate is blocked again by the Democratic National Committee. (As an aside, one imagines that Bernie will carry the Wisconsin Democratic primary in a landslide if the homeowners there know what's good for them. More than a few Republicans will probably cross over in that primary election just to guarantee a Bernie win in that race. Even the bluest of "bleu" Cheeseheads most likely go white in the face at the prospect of Molotov cocktails and burning barricades in Milwaukee come July.)

Statistics are boring, but anecdotally, it is safe to say that whereas fifty years ago Catholics as a voting bloc were a lock to vote overwhelmingly for the Democrats, now because of that party's hard-left swing on social issues on the one hand and Trump's success in wooing a good percentage of Labor Catholics away from them on the other, the Catholic vote is set to go for the Republicans on a massive scale in 2020.

How could it be otherwise? This is no longer your daddy's Democratic Party. Catholic Democrats have to decide if they are leaving the party or if the party left them. Many, like the authors, asked and answered that question years, even decades ago; many more are doing so now. The Republicans may have made it difficult in years past by being perceived as the party that was for Wall Street to the detriment of the average working man, but that is less and less the case today, especially in recent decades as the Democrats have been, if anything, just as Big Money connected/dependent. Just ask any Bernie supporter. (And, in any case, there is the *I* for Independent designation.) But regardless, Donald Trump has flipped that longstanding narrative, and the Trump brand of Republicanism is reshaping the American political landscape.

Social Issues of Particular Importance to Catholics

A strange fanaticism fills our time: the fanatical hatred of morality, especially of Christian morality.[4]

G. K. Chesterton

The 2016 election was a critical one for Catholics in the United States of America. Practicing Catholics know that the Democrats' stand on social issues like abortion has been at odds with Church teaching and basic morality for a long time. Hence, there has been a gradual migration of many from the political party of their forefathers as they could not reconcile the conflict. However, many Catholics, and practically all of them in high public office, have chosen to compromise their supposed or professed moral beliefs in order to continue to support the party that their family has always supported. They rationalized that disconnect for many years by their native disagreement with the Republicans on economic issues and by taking refuge in the "personally

---

[4]   "Quotations of G. K. Chesterton," *The Apostolate of Common Sense*, https://www.chesterton.org/quotations-of-g-k-chesterton/.

opposed but don't want to impose my morality" dodge. (We say "dodge" because all law is an imposition of morality on someone who may disagree. If we want to drive one hundred miles per hour in a school zone, society imposes its morality on us.)

Sadly, over the course of time, many people came to prioritize their "identity" as Democrats over their identity as Catholics. Tragically, that loyalty to the Democratic Party has been the solvent in which the faith lives of innumerable Catholics, many prominent politicians among them, have dissolved.

One thing that changed with the 2016 election is the Democrats' increasingly obvious embrace of the most radical expressions of things with which most Catholics, to say nothing of other people of good will, are at the very least uncomfortable. The mask is off for all to see. In truth, it has been for some time, but there seems to be an increased urgency among the Democrats to make anyone with the slightest vestigial attachment to traditional Christian morality uncomfortable.

One could say that those controlling the donkey party became radicalized slowly at first, and then all of a sudden. Witness how quickly the change in the view of normative human sexuality has occurred. It seems like just yesterday that civil unions—not gay marriage mind you, civil unions—were being hotly debated in places like Massachusetts and Vermont. Fast forward to today and Elizabeth Warren informs us that whomever she nominates to be her secretary of education will be interviewed and vetted by a nine-year-old trans student. What? And she tells us that the prison in which a man who thinks he is a woman is incarcerated is one of the most important issues facing us today! So much for "It's the economy, stupid." Apparently in 2020, it is trans convict housing.

But it is not just that they are crazy. That would be merely humorous if their craziness did not have such tragic consequences and did not affect our lives. What, one wonders, caused so many old-school Catholic Labor Democrats to vote for Trump in 2016 and probably will, and certainly should, cause many more, including Hispanics, to do so in 2020? Catholic Democrats got "woke." That is what happened. Not "woke" in the normal parlance of that cool new term (look it up if you have to), but they woke up to the craziness of the Democrats at the national level as reflected in the truly evil nature of their views on life issues and the increasingly totalitarian nature of their views vis-à-vis religious freedom. In addition to the absolute hostility of the Democrat leadership to traditional Christianity, many Catholic Democrats also woke up to the fact that Donald Trump is, in fact, closer to their beliefs on economic matters and foreign policy than anyone that either party would put forward from their "establishments." Donald Trump was and is the Republican candidate who, in a sense, gave them permission to leave the reservation. One wonders if 2020 will be the year in which Kristen Day and the millions like her finally take "no" for an answer.[5]

---

[5]   Given the tenor of an opinion piece she later wrote, it appears that this is the year. Kristen Day, "Kristen Day: Buttigieg and 2020 hopefuls, don't cancel 21 million pro-life Dems if you want to beat Trump," *Fox News*, February 7, 2020, https://www.foxnews.com/opinion/buttigieg-2020-21-million-pro-life-dems-beat-trump.

The 2016 election was, and this is no exaggeration, a true tipping point in the moral direction of our country. Simply put, if Hillary Clinton had won, the ability of Catholics to practice and live the faith would have been increasingly curtailed. Democrat dogma demands it. As the normalization of the most extreme abortion rights views and the most intolerant "tolerance enforcement" of the LGBTQ agenda proceeded apace, consider how much religious freedom has been lost already and how much more would have been had the radical Democrats retained power.

Catholic organizations, like Catholic Charities in Boston a number of years ago, have been driven from the adoption process for not being willing to place children with homosexual couples. With the passage of Obamacare and its contraception mandate, the Little Sisters of the Poor (the Little Sisters of the Poor for crying out loud!) and other groups had to go to court to be allowed not to violate their consciences by offering contraceptive coverage. President Trump has expressed his support for the Sisters in both word and deed.

Following are thoughts on Donald Trump in light of some particular issues that should loom large in the decision-making process of any Catholic when it comes time to vote. In truth, that is what the entire book is about, but abortion and religious freedom bear special mention.

Abortion

Let all the babies be born. Then let us drown those we do not like.[6]

G. K. Chesterton

When G. K. Chesterton, that great "apostle of common sense," wrote these words, he was making a point at a time when nobody would even consider doing such a thing, or at least would recognize it for the barbarism that it is. Would that he could have foreseen the future (perhaps he did) and glimpsed today's moral landscape when that willingness to condone, even celebrate as a sacred right, the killing of the most innocent and defenseless among us is precisely the stance of a not insignificant number of prominent Democrats, albeit drowning is not the preferred method. A few inches difference in one direction or another in the birth canal does not make a dime's worth, nor does the argument that late term abortions are rare, which may be true percentage wise but not in terms of numbers. One is too many once you see it for what it is.

The sheer willingness to condone it is horrifying, as is the extent to which some individuals will take this so-called right to choose. Witness the disgusting sentiments expressed by the governor of Virginia regarding infanticide as President Trump rightly called it. Consider that the Democratic Party's very platform supports unrestricted abortion up to the moment of birth; are we Catholics supposed to subsidize this barbarism? The Democrats truly are, as Trump labels

---

[6]   G. K. Chesterton, "Babies and Distributism," *GK's Weekly*, November 12, 1932.

them, "the party of third-trimester abortion." But enough of the depths to which the Democrats have sunk. What of President Trump?

On abortion, the killing of the unborn child in the womb, Donald Trump had some catching up to do. He was not a lifelong pro-lifer. He has not traditionally been thought of as a particularly religious man. And yet, for whatever reason, he has been the best friend the unborn around the world have had in the oval office since *Roe v. Wade*. He pledged to name pro-life justices, and he has done so. One strong one in Neil Gorsuch and another, though perhaps to a lesser degree it seems, in Brett Kavanaugh. If elected to a second term, the president will, perhaps, fill still another seat.

And it is not just at the Supreme Court level; he has in effect remade the federal judiciary by naming nearly two hundred judges, the vast majority of whom one can expect will respect the Constitution and be friendly to the pro-life cause and religious freedom.

He was the first president to directly address the March for Life, the annual gathering of hundreds of thousands of pro-lifers, young and old, to demonstrate and pray for an end to abortion, an event the true size of which the main-stream media has minimized and blacked out for years. There, he gave a stirring speech and made unequivocal his and his administration's commitment to rolling back the pro-abortion efforts of prior administrations.

He has spoken out more directly to the media about their own support for abortion. Witness when he turned the tables on MSNBC anchor and Catholic Chris Matthews. Matthews was attempting to trap candidate Trump on the question of the criminalization of abortion; instead, he was put on the spot himself, as the interviewee became the interviewer when Trump insistently asked Matthews why, if he was a Catholic, he supported abortion. He called him out in a way we've not seen a bishop do, which is a tragic thing to note by the way.[7]

These are only some of President Trump's efforts on behalf of the pro-life cause.

- Since his first day in office, President Trump has taken historic action to protect the sanctity of every American life.

- President Trump has urged Congress to pass legislation banning the horrendous practice of late-term abortion.

- Last year, President Trump took action to end Federal research using fetal tissue from abortions.

- Shortly after taking office, President Trump issued a memorandum reinstating and expanding the Mexico City Policy, banning funding to organizations that provide abortion overseas.

- The Trump Administration issued a rule preventing Title X family planning funds from supporting the abortion industry.

- President Trump became the first sitting president to address the annual March for Life rally.[8]

---

[7]   For a more complete detailing of Trump's pro-life accomplishments, please see appendix 1 at the back of the book.

[8]   "President Donald J. Trump Is Devoted To Protecting American Freedoms and Promoting American Values," The White House, February 4, 2020, https://www.whitehouse.gov/briefings-state ments/president-donald-j-trump-is-devoted-to-protecting-ameri can-freedoms-and-promoting-american-values/.

It is not only the question of abortion, however, on which the choice for Catholics could not be more clear. The actual right to freely practice our faith seems to be, by all indications, past events, official positions, and public statements, in conflict with the principles of the Democratic Party and the entire drift of the culture under their administration.

Human Sexuality and Religious Freedom

Religious liberty might be supposed to mean that everybody is free to discuss religion. In practice it means that hardly anybody is allowed to mention it.[9]

G. K. Chesterton

Chesterton did not know the half of it; then again, maybe he did. G. K. had something of the prophet about him. For our entire adult reading lives, the question of the place of religion in the "public square" has been a hot topic of debate in many journals; one prominent example of which was founded with the stated goal of advocating for a place in that space. Many of our best writers have boldly taken pen in hand and written learned, erudite, and largely unread essays and books on the subject. And all during this time, ground has been lost. One would like to call it a valiant rear guard action, but in truth, it has been a rout. And then, just when all looked lost, off in the distance the faint sounds of

---

9   G. K. Chesterton, "The Shadow of the Sword," in *The Autobiography of G. K. Chesterton.*

a bugle were heard. Was it? Could it be? The cavalry coming to the rescue?

It was, but the commander of that cavalry was Donald Trump, and so our intellectual and religious elite rejected him at first because he was . . . what, coarse? Because he was on his third marriage? Do such people not have friends and relatives who have complicated marital histories? Because he once clotheslined Vince McMahon at a WrestleMania event and then shaved the WWE impresario's hair? The people who rejected Donald Trump were all too willing to believe the very worst of the man. It was as if Custer, at the very moment of his fabled last stand, had declined the assistance of a detachment sent to rescue him and his troops because the guy in charge of the relief force was known to darken a saloon once in a while, a poor analogy in all truth, for Trump has never had a drop in his life!

It may be safely assumed that General Custer—had he begun to disparage the newly arrived friendly forces and then dismiss them saying, "I've got this!"—would have been overruled by his troops, at least by those who had not yet been scalped. Similarly, the Never Trumpers were overruled by the Deplorables on election day 2016.

The man who was characterized as too crude, too profane, too bombastic, too whatever by the "Knights of the Keyboard," as Ted Williams contemptuously referred to the sportswriters of his day, has turned out to be the cavalry leader that religious people in this country needed all along; the problem was we were looking in all the wrong places. Apparently, he was not to be found in the editorial offices and think tanks or in the halls of Congress or in the chanceries. No, he was found on reality TV of all places. God truly does work in mysterious ways.

The fact is that Donald Trump has turned out to be as staunch a defender of religious liberty in the United States as we could hope for in this era.

In addition to the achievements with regards to abortion already detailed and expanded upon in appendix 1, consider the Trump administration's concrete results related to religious freedom on the domestic front:

- In 2017, President Trump signed an executive order to advance religious freedom, restoring the ideals that have undergirded our Nation since its founding.
- The President took action to ensure Americans and organizations are not forced to violate their religious or moral beliefs by complying with Obamacare's contraceptive mandate.
- The Department of Health and Human Services (HHS) established a new Conscience and Religious Freedom division to help direct the agency's efforts to protect religious freedom.
- HHS took action to protect the right of healthcare entities to act according to their conscience.
- This year, the Administration finalized a rule providing more flexibility for Federal employees whose religious beliefs require them to abstain from work on certain days.
- The Administration has unequivocally stood for religious freedom in the courts.[10]

---

[10]   "President Trump is Committed to Protecting Religious Freedom

While President Trump has been very active and solicitous in seeking to protect religious freedom, he is not Catholic. With regards to an issue such as gay marriage, he cannot be said to hold the Catholic view, as he seems not as concerned about the normalization of homosexual relations, but, truth be told, if we are realists, we must acknowledge that that ship has sailed for the foreseeable future. As you will see in the list of accomplishments in the appendix, the author of that list includes the naming of homosexual ambassadors and working to exercise leverage on foreign nations to get them to decriminalize homosexual acts.

That acknowledged, it is the Catholic position that any sexual activity outside of marriage between a man and a woman is sinful; it is not the Church's position that consenting sexual acts, whether heterosexual or homosexual in nature, should be criminalized. But it is true that Trump, at least politically, is not "with" the Church on same-sex marriage and seems to consider it settled law, but he is much better than anyone the Democrats will put forward and just as good as the best Republican in terms of what can actually be accomplished. In fact, he is probably better, for he has demonstrated the courage and political ability to carve out a solid space for religious freedom and to nominate the types of judges who may look at some of the judicial activism by which much past mischief was done with a jaundiced eye.

Under the previous administration, one would have to

---

in the United States and Around the World," The White House, September, 23, 2019, https://www.whitehouse.gov/briefings -statements/president-trump-committed-protecting-religious -freedom-united-states-around-world/.

be blind not to have noticed a creeping totalitarianism in opposition to traditional Christian values, so much so that it increasingly seemed we were allowed to let those beliefs and values inform the way in which we live our lives, organize our parochial schools, and conduct our charitable activities only to the extent that *they*, "the tolerance police," saw fit. Under Trump, we have a fighting chance to be allowed to raise our children and carry out our charitable works as *we* see fit. If you don't believe us, this may be a good time to read or re-read Father Pavone's outstanding foreword. That tells the tale from a first-person perspective.

Even less-active and non-practicing Catholics of our acquaintance seem to acknowledge that the Left continues to push and push the most radical positions; both authors know many Catholic Democrats and Independents who are fans of Donald Trump as a result of the radicalism of the Democrats.

Still, we Catholics can appeal to President Trump to respect those traditional societies that have not yet succumbed to the LGBTQ propaganda and pressure campaign for same-sex marriage against the will of the people, for remember, that momentous social change was effected judicially not legislatively in most, if not all, places. The LGBTQ pressure movement is as much a part of globalism as anything else. There is a difference between support for decriminalization and pressure to overturn cultural norms of traditional marriage against the will of the people.

The Role of Judges and Those Whom Trump Is Appointing

And finally, as alluded to earlier, in the fight for religious freedom and the fight for life, Donald Trump is accomplishing great things on the judicial front. Capably aided and advised by outstanding pro-life Catholics such as Leonard Leo, he has succeeded to date in getting almost two hundred solid constitutionalists seated in the federal judiciary. These men and women and the others he will nominate going forward will play a significant role in protecting life, as well as our freedom to be Catholics, to raise our families as we see fit, and to have a space in the public square. In comparison with what is on offer by the Democrats . . . well, never mind, there is no comparison.

The Speech

In 2016, Donald Trump addressed a massive crowd at a campaign rally in Florida. An abbreviated version of that speech has been edited and set to music and circulates the internet under the title "This Speech Will Get Donald Trump Elected," and it did, or at least the ideas expressed in it found an enthusiastic audience across the country.

This well-edited video excerpt from the longer speech that day in Florida is an inspiring masterpiece of political rhetoric as he hit upon his major points unabashedly and unapologetically, calling out the "corrupt political establishment" in general and the Clinton machine in particular. Here is the URL to that speech, or it may be easier or more reliable to simply search for "this speech will get Donald Trump elected": https://www.youtube.com/watch?v=szaKnOhJbow&t.

> OUR movement is about replacing a failed and corrupt political establishment with a new government controlled by you, the American people. The Washington establishment, and the financial and media corporations that fund it, exists for only one reason: to protect and enrich itself.
>
> The establishment has trillions of dollars at stake in this election. For those who control the levers of power in Washington and for the global special interests they partner with, these people that don't have your good in mind.
>
> Our campaign represents a true, existential threat like they haven't seen before. This is not simply another four-year election. This is a crossroads in the history of our civilization that will determine whether or not we, the people, reclaim control over our government.
>
> The political establishment that is trying to stop us is the same group responsible for our disastrous trade deals, massive illegal immigration, and economic and foreign policies that have bled our country dry.
>
> The political establishment has brought about the destruction of our factories and our jobs, as they flee to Mexico, China, and other countries all around the world.
>
> It's a global power structure that is responsible for the economic decisions that have robbed our working class, stripped our country of its wealth, and put that money into the pockets of a handful of large corporations and political entities.
>
> This is a struggle for the survival of our nation, and this

will be our last chance to save it. This election will determine whether we're a free nation or whether we have only the illusion of democracy but are in fact controlled by a small handful of global special interests rigging the system, and our system is rigged. This is reality. You know it, they know it, I know it, and pretty much the whole world knows it. The Clinton Machine is at the center of this power structure. . . .

. . . We've seen this firsthand in the WikiLeaks documents in which Hillary Clinton meets in secret with international banks to plot the destruction of US sovereignty in order to enrich these global, financial powers, her special interest friends, and her donors.

Honestly, she should be locked up. The most powerful weapon deployed by the Clintons is the corporate media, the press. Let's be clear on one thing: the corporate media in our country is no longer involved in journalism.

They're a political, special interest no different than any lobbyist or other financial entity, with a total political agenda, and the agenda is not for you; it's for themselves.

Anyone who challenges their control is deemed a sexist, a racist, a xenophobe. They will lie, lie, lie, and then again, they will do worse than that. They will do whatever's necessary. The Clintons are criminals. Remember that.

This is well-documented, and the establishment that protects them has engaged in a massive cover-up of widespread criminal activity at the State Department and the Clinton Foundation in order to keep the Clintons in power.

They knew they would throw every lie they could at me and my family and my loved ones. They knew they would stop at nothing to try to stop me. Nevertheless, I take all of these slings and arrows gladly for you. I take them for our movement so that we can have our country back.

I knew this day would arrive. It was only a question of when, and I knew the American people would rise above it and vote for the future they deserve.

The only thing that can stop this corrupt machine is you. The only force strong enough to save our country is us. The only people brave enough to vote out this corrupt establishment is you, the American people. Our great civilization has come upon a moment of reckoning.

I didn't need to do this, folks, believe me. I built a great company and I had a wonderful life. I could've enjoyed the fruits and benefit of years of successful business deals and businesses for myself and my family instead of going through this absolute horror show of lies, deceptions, malicious attacks. Who would've thought? I'm doing it because this country has given me so much and I feel so strongly that it's my turn to give back to the country that I love.

I'm doing this for the people and for the movement, and we will take back this country for you, and we will make America great again.[11]

---

[11]   Transcript of "Speech that made Trump President," Trollitics, video, 5:37, November 9, 2016, https://www.youtube.com/watch?v=szaKnOhJbow&t=.

1

L O V E

The greatest of these is love.

1 Corinthians 13:13

Wow. What a group. What a group. Thank you. Thank you very much. Thank you, folks. Thank you, folks. It's great to be right here in Florida, which we love.[1]

THESE sentences were uttered by Trump at the beginning of that speech, but it is not included in the edited video version, the transcript of which you just read. Why begin here? After all, this is just the standard acknowledgment of applause anyone offers at the beginning of a speech, along with a who knows how sincere, seemingly standard political claim to love those in the audience. Right?

But do you know what? Donald Trump is sincere. He does love Florida and Floridians as he loves America and Americans, the average ones, not just those who "count" or the special interests. In fact, that is what is most striking about his remarkable campaign and unlikely victory: the palpable,

---

[1] "Speech: Donald Trump – West Palm Beach, FL – October 13, 2016," Factbase Videos, video, 46:36, October 23, 2017, https:// youtu.be/RSw0yMFuPRk.

genuine, obvious, and very real love that exists between that man and the people who turn out in the tens and hundreds of thousands to cheer him on.

Trump is a man who loves deeply—his family, his country, his supporters, and, yes, we believe, God. Why else would he have sacrificed so much, subjected himself and his family to the vicious assaults of the media and the opposition party— and they have been vicious—stood strong in the face of the absurd and discredited accusations of collusion with Russia, the manufactured impeachment attempt which failed miserably, and the attempted ongoing coup which is in the process of being revealed by Inspector General Horowitz, Attorney General Barr, and US Attorney Durham.

This love is no opportunistic one either. It is so patently *real*, unlike that species of love so transparently and awkwardly espoused by so many politicians. Everything about Donald John Trump shows his love for the little man, the "average Joe," regardless of the lies about him peddled by the elite, a class to which he belongs by virtue of his wealth and among which he can move but with which he has limited sympathy. No, this is a man of the people, upon whom the coastal elites and the political class look down. (If you doubt that assertion, look up his old WWE clips online. The Donald has always had "the common touch" it seems.) Exhibit A in support of the depth of that love could be simply the fervent way in which it is reciprocated.

The Trump rallies have become a cultural phenomenon unto themselves, both in-person and on television. When he is there, in front of tens of thousands of his supporters, he is in his element. His political betters mock him and call him "unpresidential." And in one sense, they are right. He is unpresidential and unlike any politician we have seen in recent memory because he tells it like it is; he calls 'em as he sees 'em, to use a baseball phrase. He does not rely on focus groups and tested messaging to deceive the people he loves. He loves them too much to do that.

But with world leaders, he is certainly presidential and then some. Honestly observe his interactions with them. He quickly establishes a rapport, and there seems to be a genuine respect and affection between Donald Trump and many of his counterparts. Did you see any coverage of his trip to India or any of his other official visits? Of course, there are those whom one could describe as his political adversaries. Still, even with them, he is eminently presidential. This is a leader of men who can move effectively in very different worlds and on different stages. He knows that a Trump rally is not the same environment as an official state dinner.

Recall that after Obamacare was passed, one of the architects of that bill for the Obama administration was caught on video saying at a panel discussion, "Lack of transparency is a huge political advantage, . . . call it the stupidity of the American voter or whatever, but basically that was really, really critical for the thing to pass."[2]

That is not how you deal with a public you claim to love. No. You tell them the truth, and Trump has been telling the truth about American politics for as long as he has been in

---

2   Elise Viebeck, "ObamaCare architect: 'Stupidity' of voters helped bill pass," *The Hill*, November 10, 2014, https://thehill.com/pol icy/healthcare/223578-obamacare-architect-lack-of-transparency -helped-law-pass.

public life. Look up old interviews of him from the '80s. His "talking points" were the same back then because they are not talking points. They are deeply held beliefs rooted in a solid grasp of global economic and political realities. He saw the disaster of the last few decades and the hollowing out of American manufacturing and prestige coming. Undoubtedly, he also knew what awaited the working class of this country.

2

MAIN STREET VERSUS WALL STREET

Everyone should be able to draw from work the
means of providing for his life and that of his family,
and of serving the human community.

Catechism of the Catholic Church 2428

The political establishment that is trying to stop us is the same
group responsible for our disastrous trade deals, massive ille-
gal immigration, and economic and foreign policies that have
bled our country dry. The political establishment has brought
about the destruction of our factories and our jobs, as they flee
to Mexico, China, and other countries all around the world.[1]

PERHAPS no other aspect of his campaign and his presidency
captures the genuine love that Donald Trump has for the
American people than his approach to the economy and his
relentless drive to restore the possibility of prosperity for all

---

[1]   Transcript of "Speech that made Trump President," Trollitics,
video, 5:37, November 9, 2016, https://www.youtube.com/
watch?v=szaKnOhJbow&t=.

of the nation's citizens. As these words are being written, the Democrat House managers are making their case to impeach the president in the United States Senate chambers. In stark juxtaposition, President Trump was just in Davos, Switzerland telling the World Economic Forum that his prescription of America First is working here and can work for other countries as well, that the global economic construct has favored a global economic elite (the very people he is speaking to) at the expense of the citizens of each and every country. To double down on two overwrought and overused phrases in the same sentence, Trump is speaking truth to power in the belly of the beast, and doing so in his own inimitable way and incredibly successfully. When Donald Trump speaks on the economy and trade and manufacturing, he is truly on home turf, no matter what country he happens to be in at the time. The old adage "It's the economy, stupid!" (reportedly coined by Bill Clinton advisor James Carville) coupled with his ability to articulate the problem and solution was, in fact, the real key to his victory.

In places like coal country—where Hillary had the remarkably bad judgment to talk about her war on coal— in old mill towns in New England where the opioid crisis is laying waste to the human populations still dwelling amidst the ruins, in the once humming manufacturing centers of the upper Midwest that now are part of the all too accurately named Rust Belt, and among people like those described by Michael Moore—"Joe Blow, Billy Bob Blow, all the Blows"—the fact that the once great middle class of this country has been decimated under both Republican and Democrat administrations over the last few decades, with moments here and there when it seemed they had a fighting chance, made Trump's message of rebuilding the manufacturing base of the country, keeping us out of trade "deals" that enriched Wall Street at the expense of Main Street, revamping the tax code, and cutting much onerous regulation, gave hope to so many for whom that virtue has, understandably, been in short supply for many years.

One of the most insightful and well-informed commentators on the Trump administration's economic policies and the current drama unfolding in our country goes by the moniker of Sundance and writes at the blog *The Last Refuge*. Based on various posts made around Christmas and Easter each year by a contributor called Menagerie, one wonders if Sundance himself is not a Catholic. Here he explains in layman's terms how Trump differs from the average American politician of both parties:

> The strongest argument against the U.S. trade and economic policies of the past 30 years has been the outcome. We don't need to guess what the pros and cons of the U.S. Chamber of Commerce position is, we are living them. We don't need to guess what the Wall Street economy delivers, we are living through them.
>
> For the past 30 years the U.S. has lost jobs, wages have been depressed, and the middle-class has suffered through the implementation of economic trade policy that destroyed the U.S. manufacturing base. None of this is in question – the results stare us in the face – yet the Wall Street and multinational corporate club(s)

(U.S. CoC chief among them) now demand a contin-
uance of the same.

The economic and trade policies of the Trump
administration are adverse to those interests. As we
have shared for several years, candidate Trump, now
President Trump is an existential threat to the multinational program.[2]

Read that first paragraph again. It quite simply states,
in different words, that the establishment has no clothes
when it comes to the American economy. The "experts"
of both parties have told us for thirty years and more that
the globally-oriented trade deals were "win-wins," that any
high-paying manufacturing or mining jobs could be easily
replaced through "re-training" or by an exciting job in the
new "service" economy—which often, in practice, meant
waiting tables or serving as a customer service representative
for ten dollars an hour—that the shuttering of the factory
in your town as production moved to Mexico or China was
all part of the glorious process of free trade, a part known as
"creative destruction." Anyone driving through the former
industrial areas of our country could be forgiven for thinking that what we got was a bit heavy on the destruction and
a bit lean on the creative. For those old enough to remember
the Billy Joel song "Allentown," that told the story pretty
well. Give it a listen, perhaps especially if you are not old

---

2   Sundance, "Prepare—MAGAnomics Is The Battle—The Res-
      toration of a Balanced Economy is The Goal," The Last Refuge
      (blog), March 1, 2018, https://theconservativetreehouse.com/
      2018/03/01/prepare-maganomics-is-the-battle-the-restoration-of
      -a-balanced-economy-is-the-goal/.

enough to remember it. It paints a vividly depressing picture of the loss of good steel industry jobs, the resultant growth of a welfare environment, the damage such an environment does to a man's soul, and the havoc it wreaks on families.

The economy under which the average American has suffered and seen his standard of living decline in recent decades is a construct against which Donald Trump has waged rhetorical war for thirty years. In short, Donald J. Trump is for the American working class, plain and simple. Yes, he is rich; yes, he is ostentatious; yes, he flaunts his wealth and all that flows from it,—yes, yes, yes, a thousand times yes—and yet he truly loves the working man and woman. As does the Catholic Church.

The Catholic Church in the United States was, for many years, *the* champion of the laboring class, a fact that stood to reason both because the vast majority of ethnic Catholics that came to this country were part of that working class and because the Catholic Church, through the application of Christ's teaching as expressed in the Church's authentic social doctrine, has, when listened to, served as a leaven in every society in which she is present, a leaven that has always and everywhere served to ameliorate the suffering of the poor, if often imperfectly.

Certainly, Catholics well-versed in the finer points of that social doctrine can and do disagree as to how best to implement it or, more accurately, apply its principles in a given society.

What is striking to many observers, however, is how, over the years, one of two "systems" opposed by the Church have come to be embraced by many Catholics. In a kind of diabolical "either/or," socialism or unrestrained capitalism—or an unhealthy combination of the two in the form of neoliberalism garnished with the worst type of crony capitalism and a vast welfare state—seem to be the choices we are offered by the political establishment. The Church condemns both of the principal flawed systems; here is how she does so in the *Catechism*:

> The Church has rejected the totalitarian and atheistic ideologies associated in modern times with "communism" or "socialism." She has likewise refused to accept, in the practice of "capitalism," individualism and the absolute primacy of the law of the marketplace over human labor. Regulating the economy solely by centralized planning perverts the basis of social bonds; regulating it solely by the law of the marketplace fails social justice, for "there are many human needs which cannot be satisfied by the market." Reasonable regulation of the marketplace and economic initiatives, in keeping with a just hierarchy of values and a view to the common good, is to be commended.[3]

Full-throated socialism embodied by Bernie Sanders— almost solely on the national scene for a number of years and now reinforced by "the squad" of Alexandria Ocasio-Cortes et al—is making a comeback in the Democratic Party in response to the globalist free-trading/socialist-lite/managerial state "centrist" wing of the party, embodied in the last election by Hillary Clinton. Hence, most Catholics who

---

[3]   CCC 2425.

remain in the Democratic Party have been converted over the years to one of these positions.

But lest the establishment Republicans—many of whom are, or at least were, Never Trumpers—try to claim the mantle of the exclusive party of Catholic social teaching, they, on the other hand, have gotten away with parroting the "global free-trade" talking points and had been converted to an almost worshipful adulation of the "invisible hand." They opposed Trump on the economy every chance they could; they supported the trade deals that gutted the rust belt and other places; they would lecture him during the 2016 campaign and later as to why tariffs don't work; some opposed his nomination for trade representative, Robert Lighthizer, a name you should know, for he is the man who spearheaded negotiations on the greatest trade deals this country has ever seen: the United States Mexico Canada Agreement (USMCA) to replace NAFTA and the China trade deal. Maybe the establishment Republicans were not as smart as they thought they were. To their credit, many have become strong supporters of Trump as they see his policies working in real time.

Clearly, Donald Trump is no socialist, though he does, like the Church, acknowledge a role for the state in the regulation of the economy. For confirmation of that, one need only take a cursory glance at appendix 2, which is a list of his accomplishments. Even a passing look at the list would make clear that, as president, Trump is not averse to a role, even a relatively robust one, for the state compared to a libertarian position. Those who claim that by slashing regulations, Trump is some type of radical free-marketeer are either willfully ignorant or honestly don't realize that regulations which make it impossible for small Main Street businesses to compete with the "big boys" or for a vitally needed bridge to be built inside of ten years need to be looked at and, quite likely, eliminated. The Church is almost always precise in her teachings such that you can frequently identify a key qualifying word in a sentence. What is the key word in the following passage from the *Catechism*? "Reasonable regulation of the marketplace and economic initiatives, in keeping with a just hierarchy of values and a view to the common good, is to be commended." Give up? One key word, at least with regards to regulation, is "reasonable."

Trump does not seek to strip away any and all regulations. That he is removing eight (or is it up to thirteen now?) for every one that is added is indicative of how over-regulated our economy was rather than how radical he is. All indications point to an attitude toward regulation that is in keeping with Church teaching. He acknowledges a role for the state, but burdensome regulations have hamstrung, if not crippled, many aspects of the economy and the common wealth for years. The Trump administration's efforts to remove the burdensome regulations have loosed the reins, and investment is flowing back into the United States—yes, aided by those pesky tariffs that we were told by the worshippers of the disastrous trade deals of past years would never work. Well, they were wrong; the tariffs are working just fine. The United States has a lot of leverage in its trade negotiations with other countries. Trump, for some reason, is our first politician in many years to actually use that leverage to help the people who elected him.

We could continue to unpack this passage from the *Catechism*: ". . . in keeping with a just hierarchy of values and view to the common good." A just hierarchy of values, from a Catholic point of view, would prioritize the ability of families to support themselves rather than be dependent upon the government. This is not the place for an attack on the welfare state which has arisen, almost as a necessity one could argue, in response to the gutting of America's manufacturing base and economic wastelands in its inner cities.[4] No, but it is the place to ask if the economy which the establishment has given us has derived from a "just hierarchy of values and a view to the common good." Or, rather, has it resulted from an unjust or disordered hierarchy of values and a view to the particular good of some relatively few "winners"? Wall Street versus Main Street. Call it ironic if you will that the champion of Main Street over and against the interest of Wall Street is, perhaps, the most famous billionaire in the world.

Again, Sundance:

> Think about it. *Big Picture.*
>
> Donald Trump is focused, intensely focused, on Main Street – not Wall Street. The era of Main Street, middle-class, American economics becoming the primary interest of economic policy is right now. . . .
>
> This is a fundamental paradigm shift. A conversation about what is the *best play* for a Main Street

---

[4]   Of course, the collapse of the family and other societal problems play their role as well. One could also argue that the welfare state itself creates a self-perpetuating cycle that incentivizes its continuation and growth by inhibiting the formation of families. But, again, this is not the place for that discussion.

corporation, which has direct impact on middle-class jobs.

This is exactly what candidate Trump said he was going to do. Don't get caught up in the media obfuscation, accept it for what it is.

It is not a simple feat to untangle the multi-decade web of corporate outsourcing for profit (Wall Street). Many would say it is an impossible task, but we did not elect *many*, we elected the one man who said that is exactly what he is willing to do – focus intensely on Main Street economics.

There are going to be internal adverse interests who have a vested stake in global manufacturing and production benefits. Those multinational corporate interests are going to be in opposition to national economic interests, and President Trump is going to have to navigate his way through their oppositional efforts while trying to offset any negative impacts to the American people.[5]

He goes on to describe how the influence acquired by K Street (i.e., lobbyists for special interests that would frequently "buy" politicians and favorable legislation and often even write it) expanded and how Trump's Main Street centric approach is designed to destroy that corrupt model which has been in place for decades to the benefit of the few

---

5   Sundance, "Prepare—MAGAnomics Is The Battle—The Restoration of a Balanced Economy is The Goal," The Last Refuge (blog), March 1, 2018, https://theconservativetreehouse.com/2018/03/01/prepare-maganomics-is-the-battle-the-restoration-of-a-balanced-economy-is-the-goal/.

and the detriment of many. Sundance, in what amounts to a mini-course in MAGAnomics explains:

> Removal of regulation and empowering full utilization of energy resources is the quick start into the carburetor of the domestic economic engine. Using tax policy to infuse manufacturing and production with capital while making domestic long-term investment the best play for financial return is another aspect. Accelerated depreciation schedules only amplify the investment and return possibilities.
>
> The return of the Industrial Titans will also unleash true business entrepreneurship where innovation and uniquely American skills of product development are national advantages. Americans know how to think independently, often outside the box, innovation is in our national DNA.
>
> We are also blessed to have the natural resources needed to fully develop a renewed manufacturing economy. The underlying architecture and infrastructure is right here in our own back yards. The possibilities are only limited to our own imagination.
>
> However, there are adversarial interests, multinational corporations, who remain invested in the American outsourcing model. Together with foreign interests they will work to undermine any change in the current service-driven, i.e. 'dependency', economic model which they built over the past 30 years.[6]

---

[6]   Ibid.

In a later post, Sundance did a deep dive into the details of the effects on the American consumer wrought by the global economic system and examined the expected effects of President Trump's economic program over time. Sneak preview: the end result will be a shift from dependency to independence, in terms of both the national economy and the family.

His discussion of Social Security in the same post explains the general thrust of the Trump economic plan.

> To fully understand how Donald Trump views the solvency of Social Security, you must again understand his economic model and how it outlines growth.
>
> The issue with Social Security, as viewed by Trump, is more of an issue with receipts and expenditures. If the aggregate U.S. economy is growing by a factor larger than the distribution needed to fulfill its entitlement obligations, then no wholesale change on expenditure is needed. The focus needs to be on continued and successful economic growth.
>
> What you will find in all of Donald Trump's positions, is a paradigm shift he necessarily understands **must take place** in order to accomplish the long-term goals for the U.S. citizen as it relates to "entitlements" or "structural benefits".
>
> All other candidates are beginning their policy proposals with a fundamentally divergent perception of the U.S. economy. They are working with, and retaining the outlook of, a U.S. economy based on "services"; a service-based economic model.

While this economic path has been created by decades old U.S. policy, and is ultimately the only historical economic path now taught in school, Trump intends to change the course entirely.

Because so many shifts—policy nudges—have taken place in the past several decades, few academics and even fewer [mainstream media] observers, are able to understand how to get off this path and chart a better course.

Candidate Trump is proposing less dependence on foreign companies for cheap goods, (the cornerstone of a service economy) and a return to a more *balanced* U.S. larger economic model where the manufacturing and production base can be re-established *and competitive* based on American entrepreneurship and innovation.

The key words in the prior statement are "dependence" and "balanced". When a nation has an industrial manufacturing balance within the GDP there is far less dependence on the economic activity in global markets. In essence the U.S. can sustain itself, absorb global economic fluctuations and expand itself or contract itself depending on the free market.

When there is no balance, there is no longer a free market. The free market is sacrificed in favor of dependency, whether it's foreign oil or foreign manufacturing, the dependency outcome is essentially the same. Without balance there is an inherent loss of economic independence, and a consequential increase in economic risk.

No other economy in the world innovates like the U.S.A. Donald Trump sees this as a key advantage across all industry—including manufacturing and technology.

The benefit of cheap overseas labor, which is considered a global market disadvantage for the U.S., is offset by utilizing innovation and energy independence.

The third highest variable cost of goods beyond raw materials first, and labor second, is energy. If the U.S. energy sector is unleashed—and fully developed—the manufacturing price of any given product will allow for global trade competition even with higher U.S. wage prices.

In addition the U.S. has a key strategic advantage with raw manufacturing materials such as: iron ore, coal, steel, precious metals and vast mineral assets which are needed in most new modern era manufacturing. Trump proposes we stop selling these valuable national assets to countries we compete against—they belong to the American people, they should be used for the benefit of American citizens. Period. . . .

When you combine FULL resource development (in a modern era) with the removal of over-burdensome regulatory and compliance systems, necessarily filled with enormous bureaucratic costs, Donald Trump proposes we can lower the cost of production and be globally competitive. In essence, Trump changes the economic paradigm, and we no longer become a dependent nation relying on a service driven economy.

. . .

In addition, an unquantifiable benefit comes from investment, where the smart money play—to get increased return on investment—becomes putting capital INTO the U.S. economy, instead of purchasing foreign stocks.

With all of the above opportunities in mind, this is how we get on the pathway to rebuilding our national infrastructure. The demand for labor increases, and as a consequence so too does the U.S. wage rate which has been stagnant (or non-existent) for the past three decades.

As the wage rate increases, and as the economy expands, the governmental dependency model is reshaped and simultaneously receipts to the U.S. treasury improve.

More money into the U.S. Treasury and less dependence on welfare/social service programs have a combined exponential impact. You gain a dollar, and have no need to spend a dollar—the saved sum is doubled. That is how the SSI and safety net programs are saved under President Trump.

When you elevate your economic thinking, you begin to see that all of the "entitlements" or expenditures become more affordable with an economy that is fully functional.

As the GDP of the U.S. expands, so does our ability to meet the growing need of the retiring U.S. worker. We stop thinking about how to best divide a limited economic pie, and begin thinking about how many more economic pies we can create.

Simply put, we begin to….

…..Make America Great Again![7]

If you, as a self-described Catholic Democrat, are rabidly pro-abortion or if the promotion of the LGBTQ agenda and the normalization of things like drag queen story hour loom large in your list of vital issues to support, you probably don't care that much about all of the above. You will never vote for Trump or anyone like him as long as the Democrats continue to trot out candidates like this year's roster of radicals in their primary.

But if you are an old-fashioned Catholic Labor or Hispanic Democrat, not particularly enthused about the Democratic Party platform with respect to that stuff, if you are a Catholic Democrat because your parents were and their parents before them and because the Democrats were once the party of the union and the working man, well then, what do you disagree with in this chapter? Donald Trump is your man. He is fighting for you and your family. The economic results of his first term speak for themselves.

A request for the president: Dear Mr. President, your unique brand of MAGAnomics is reaping great benefits for America's working class, but we would like to hear more mention of support for stay-at-home moms. Mr. President, please consider vocalizing support for the concept of single-income families. We read your economic program as being

---

7   Sundance, "Wall Street, Main Street, and Global Economics With a Donald Trump Victory…," *The Last Refuge* (blog), November 9, 2016, https://theconservativetreehouse.com/2016/11/09/wall -street-main-street-and-global-economics-with-a-donald-trump -victory/.

designed to make that possible, even if unintentionally, but you often tout as a main achievement of your administration the fact that women make up a greater percentage of the work force than ever before. It is the experience of these two Catholic husbands and fathers that many women, across the political spectrum, would love to have the option and ability to stay home with their children. You have been able to enact so many family friendly policies, but what is most often touted are things assuming a model wherein the children are in daycare.

This request is not to denigrate the talents of women nor to underestimate the "feminine genius," to use a favorite phrase of Pope St. John Paul II, but rather to celebrate and support the mothers among them in their most important role, that of mom. (Some women may take umbrage at this idea, but we doubt that any mothers will, or children for that matter.) Family life is the key to so many societal indicators of "success," and mothers in the home are a societal "good" not to be underestimated. Please, Mr. President, take that under advisement. We know this is a cultural issue and that the great American economy you are unleashing will reap many short and long-term benefits, but know that there are many, many women out there who would love, we mean love, to leave the cubicle behind and be home with their children, at least when they are young.

3

THE CORRUPT
ESTABLISHMENT

Among the deformities of the democratic system, political corruption is one of the most serious because it betrays at one and the same time both moral principles and the norms of social justice. It compromises the correct functioning of the State, having a negative influence on the relationship between those who govern and the governed. It causes a growing distrust with respect to public institutions, bringing about a progressive disaffection in the citizens with regard to politics and its representatives, with a resulting weakening of institutions. Corruption radically distorts the role of representative institutions, because they become an arena for political bartering between clients' requests and governmental services. In this way political choices favour the narrow objectives of those who possess the means to influence these choices and are an obstacle to bringing about the common good of all citizens.[1]

Compendium of the Social Doctrine of the Catholic Church
411

---

[1] Pontifical Council for Justice and Peace, *Compendium of the Social Doctrine of the Church* (Washington, DC: USCCB Publishing, 2005), no. 411, http://www.vatican.va/roman_curia/pontifical_councils/justpeace/documents/rc_pc_justpeace_doc_20060526_compendio-dott-soc_en.html#Defending peace.

*Our movement is about replacing a failed and corrupt politi-
cal establishment with a new government controlled by you, the
American people. The Washington establishment, and the financial and media corporations that fund it, exist for only one reason: to protect and enrich itself. The establishment has trillions of
dollars at stake in this election. For those who control the levers
of power in Washington and for the global special interests, they
partner with these people that don't have your good in mind.*[2]

WHAT? Corruption in Washington, DC? We are shocked, shocked we tell you! Casablanca references aside, many Americans could conceivably dismiss Trump's calling out of the "corrupt political establishment" with a shrug of the shoulders and a muttered, "What else is new? Tell us something we didn't know." The public's opinion is by now so jaded that in the mouth of any other politician, the assertion *could be* dismissed as standard boilerplate stump speech stuff.

But Trump is different. He is going after that corruption and exposing it. He is rooting it out, branch and all.

The amount and scale of the corruption that is being exposed is staggering and overwhelming, so for our purposes here, we will focus on two areas in which the political class, the establishment, has betrayed the American people: financial corruption and corruption in the legal process, or the ways in which politicians have sold their offices for personal gain and the ways in which corrupt law enforcement entities have one set of rules for "them" and another for the rest of

---

[2]   Transcript of "Speech that made Trump President," Trollitics, video, 5:37, November 9, 2016, https://www.youtube.com/watch?v=szaKnOhJbow&t=.

us. As Trump himself phrased it in the quoted passage: they exist to "protect and enrich themselves." First, the enriching.

They Came to Do Good; They Ended Up Doing Well

President Trump early and often called out the corruption of the Clinton Foundation. Increasingly, we are seeing that he was right all along. But then this is not new news. Witness a pre-2016 election article appearing on *The Hill* entitled "Clinton Foundation memo reveals Bill and Hillary as partners in crime" by Paul Jossey.

This article and those cited in the rest of this section are all stunning and should be read in their entirety. Suffice to say, they describe what can only seem to be a "pay to play" operation involving billions of dollars, multinational corporations, foreign state actors, and the State Department of the United States under Hillary Clinton and others. After detailing a number of problematic activities of the foundation, Jossey describes what he calls "the unseemly mix of . . . Teneo clients with the State Department during Ms. Clinton's tenure,"[3] Teneo being a consulting firm that served as a sort of "gatekeeper to all things Bill Clinton."

Jossey later quotes Carly Fiorina, former Republican candidate for president and no particular friend of Donald Trump, as follows: "When asked about the Clinton Global Initiative last year, Carly Fiorina stated, 'What don't we

---

[3]   Paul H. Jossey, "Clinton Foundation memo reveals Bill and Hilary as partners in crime," *The Hill*, October 31, 2016, https://thehill.com/blogs/pundits-blog/presidential-campaign/303663-bill-and-hillary-partners-in-crime-literally.

know about (Clinton Foundation) donors? What don't we know about the conflicts of interest that those donors represent when Mrs. Clinton is serving as Secretary of State?"[4]

Good questions those, and we got some answers in a scathing November 23, 2018 editorial by *Investor's Business Daily* which noted that "85 of the 154 private interests who'd met with Clinton during her tenure at state were Clinton Foundation donors."[5] But its most shocking revelation was how donations to the foundation plummeted after Hillary Clinton lost the 2016 election to Trump. "Now, fresh financial documents show that contributions and grants to the Clinton Foundation plunged since Hillary lost her election bid. They dropped from $216 million in 2016 to just $26.5 million in 2017 — a stunning 88% fall."

The editors went on to ask the right questions. They did their jobs. "If the Clinton Foundation was as good as defenders claimed, why did all its big-time donors suddenly lose interest? The only reasonable explanation is that donors weren't interested in what the foundation supposedly did for humanity. They were interested in the political favors they knew their money would buy."

Stop and think about that last sentence: *They were interested in the political favors they knew their money would buy.* Yes, we all are jaded about corruption in Washington, and to some extent, we may be resigned to a certain level of it,

---

4   Ibid.

5   Editorial, "Scam Exposed: Donations To Clinton Foundation Plummeted After Clinton Lost The Election," *Investor's Business Daily*, November 23, 2018, https://www.investors.com/politics/editorials/clinton-foundation-donations/.

but not on the scale of the corruption that transpired in the administration just before Donald Trump took office.

Not surprisingly, or perhaps surprisingly given we are talking about Washington, DC, the story was not over. A couple of weeks after the *Investor's Business Daily* editorial appeared, John Solomon wrote an article for *The Hill* entitled "Feds received whistleblower evidence in 2017 alleging Clinton Foundation wrongdoing." Solomon's article looked ahead to a then upcoming hearing:

> When a House subcommittee chairman bangs his gavel next week to convene an unprecedented investigative hearing into the Clinton Foundation, two questions will linger as preeminent: Is the Clinton family charity really the international do-gooder that earned a perfect four-star rating from Charity Navigator, or does it suffer from corruption and illegalities as conservatives allege? And if it is the latter, how much evidence of wrongdoing does the government possess? . . .
>
> The answer to the second question may reside in 6,000 pages of evidence attached to a whistleblower submission filed secretly more than a year ago with the IRS and FBI.[6]

Solomon went on to identify the investigators who filed the whistleblower submission as MDA Analytics LLC and noted that the firm alleged that the Clinton Foundation broke the

---

6   John Solomon, "Feds received whistleblower evidence in 2017 alleging Clinton Foundation wrongdoing," The Hill, December 06, 2018, https://thehill.com/opinion/white-house/420131-feds-received -whistleblower-evidence-in-2017-alleging-clinton-foundation.

law and may be liable for "millions of dollars in delinquent taxes and penalties."

Perhaps most stunning—because the phrase has become so prominent due to the impeachment process as well as the Biden/Ukraine shenanigans—was Solomon's mention of internal Clinton Foundation reviews cited by MDA in their report that "flagged serious concerns about legal compliance, improper commingling of personal and charity business and 'quid pro quo' promises made to donors while Hillary Clinton was secretary of State."

Read the last few words of that sentence again: *and "quid pro quo" promises made to donors while Hillary Clinton was secretary of State.* It truly is amazing how the Democrats constantly accuse Trump of the very things of which they themselves are guilty.

After further describing MDA's report, Solomon details how he shared the evidence with former federal investigators to assess the strength of it in terms of the potential to bring a criminal case. All of them, according to Solomon, "stressed the evidence of potential criminality was strong and warranted opening an FBI or IRS probe." One retired FBI agent was even quoted as follows: "When you have the organization's [the Clinton Foundation's] own lawyers using words like 'quid pro quo,' 'conflicts of interest' and 'whistleblower protections,' you have enough to get permission to start interviewing and asking questions."

And yet, according to Solomon, although the IRS sent multiple letters in 2017 and 2018 to MDA Analytics acknowledging receipt of the submission and noting that "it was still open and under active investigation," shortly before the 2018 election that same agency sent the firm a "preliminary denial letter indicating it did not pursue the allegations for reasons that ranged from a lack of resources to possible expiration of the statute of limitations on some of the allegations."

One could be forgiven for wondering if the fix was in. "A lack of resources" for what may be one of the largest political corruption scandals in the history of the republic? "Possible expiration of the statute of limitations on some of the allegations"? Again, one could be forgiven for suspecting that what the IRS was doing there was running out the clock. One set of rules for the powerful, another for the rest of us.

But interestingly, the story of MDA Analytics and their research into the Clinton Foundation was not over. The week after Solomon's article appeared, a hearing was scheduled to be held by a congressional subcommittee to review the work of John Huber, a special US attorney who was rumored to be investigating the Clinton foundation and other things.[7]

Attorney Huber did not appear, which was somewhat confusing, but John Moynihan and Lawrence Doyle from MDA Analytics did, and though this was a hearing that did not receive much publicity or viewership at the time, it was both fascinating and revealing.[8]

---

[7]   As this book is being prepared for publication, media reports are claiming that the Huber investigation into the Clinton Foundation is either winding down or closing entirely. News outlets favorable to the Clintons are celebrating their exoneration. Given the track record of the fake news, we are skeptical that the whole story is told, and absent official comment from the Department of Justice, we would advise them to keep the bottles of champagne corked for the time being.

[8]   You can watch it online at https://www.c-span.org/video/ ?c4767903/user-clip-john-moynihan-lawerence-w-doyle.

One reporter who did cover the story was Sara Carter.[9] She correctly identified a jaw-dropping claim when the investigators read off a list of violations or potential violations they had uncovered.

Included in the list were the following:

- foreign agent
- misrepresentations
- intentional misuse of donated public funds

Look at the first area of violation mentioned by Moynihan. Foreign agent! The family foundation of the former president of the United States and his wife, the secretary of state during some of the time under investigation, operated as a foreign agent? That is shocking and, again, invites suspicions of pay to play.

Couple that with the interesting fact that, according to Doyle, one-tenth of 1 percent of the donors donated 80 percent of the funds and it begs the question: who were those donors and what did they receive? This may be a good time to buy Peter Schweizer's *Clinton Cash* or, for a more up to date review, *Profiles in Corruption*, which is a much broader view of political families getting rich through their lives of "service."

The money quote with regards to the corruption that characterized the Clinton Foundation is captured in the following statement by Lawrence Doyle from MDA: "The

---

9   Sara Carter, "Financial Bounty Hunters Testify: Clinton Foundation Operated As Foreign Agent," December 14, 2018, https://saraacarter.com/financial-bounty-hunters-testify-clinton-foundation-operated-as-foreign-agent/.

investigation clearly demonstrates that the foundation was not a charitable organization per se, but in point of fact was a closely held family partnership. . . . As such it was governed in a fashion in which it sought in large measure to advance the personal interests of its principles."[10]

A Brief Comparison of Two Quid Pro Quos

So, there seem to have been quid pro quos aplenty in the dealings of the Clinton Foundation. Where have we heard that quaint Latin phrase recently? On the news a hundred times a day during the impeachment process, that's where. That corrupt process will be described more fully in a later chapter, but let us consider the obvious quid pro quo that was brought to light recently.

Though he is widely mocked and attacked by the majority of the mainstream media, Rudy Giuliani is uncovering, or has uncovered, a web of corruption in the Ukraine involving billions of dollars in American foreign aid that seems to have not been used for those purposes for which it was earmarked. The Ukrainians themselves say it has disappeared. And there is a major American political name involved— Biden (and some others as well)—along with certain State Department figures, including some of the witnesses in the impeachment inquiry the House held. Funny that. As was noted in a different context, certain wags online have noted that Trump is not being impeached for crimes he committed;

---

[10]   "User Clip: John Moynihan and Lawerence W. Doyle," C-SPAN, video, 1:09:36, December 14, 2018, https://www.c-span.org/video/?c4767903/user-clip-john-moynihan-lawerence-w-doyle.

the Democrats are impeaching Trump for crimes they committed, and Ukraine is ground zero of that corruption and those crimes.[11]

In the bizarro world of anti-Trump hysteria that characterizes much of the media and the mainstream political establishment, Trump was accused of soliciting a quid pro quo with the new anti-corruption president of Ukraine, Volodymyr Zelensky. He subsequently released the transcripts for all to see; if you are honest, you will see that there is no conditionality, no quid pro quo. That bears repeating: *if you are honest, you will see that there is no conditionality, no quid pro quo.* Contrast that with Joe Biden, who was caught on video bragging about his own—what any honest person recognizes as such—quid pro quo.[12]

With the flood of information that is available today online and on TV and the twenty-four-hour news cycle, it can be overwhelming to process it all. In such an environment, the average reader can trust only his own common

---

11   Incidentally, as this book goes to press, Giuliani has passed his material along to the Department of Justice—thereby exercising the right, and one might say obligation, of any American by the way who is aware of criminal behavior. As of this writing, the DOJ has reportedly established a process to evaluate and vet it.

12   For useful background reading on the subject, see Jeff Carlson, "Ukraine Accusations Against Trump Put Renewed Focus on Events During Obama Administration," The Epoch Times, October 18, 2019, https://www.theepochtimes.com/ukraine-accusations -against-trump-put-renewed-focus-on-events-during-obama -administration_3120473.html and Gregg Jarrett, "Here's Why The Justice Department Must Investigate Joe Biden's 'Quid Pro Quo,'" December 30, 2019, https://thegreggjarrett.com/heres -why-the-justice-department-must-investigate-joe-bidens-quid -pro-quo/.

sense and Occam's Razor, which holds that the simplest explanation is often the true one. In the case of Joe Biden and his son Hunter, we all read and hear the news, granted with different spins, but we all know that something is not right with the Biden story.

More and more comes out about other members of his family using the Biden family name to enrich themselves. "What about Trump and his kids?" some ask, trying to set up some type of immoral equivalence. There is no comparison. The Trump situation is perfectly legit. His children work in their father's organization, which was established long before he entered political life, while Biden's family has benefited directly from his status as a leading American politician. Just as the Clintons did through the Clinton Foundation.

If you don't think the money raked in by the Clinton Foundation was tied to her high political office, then reread that *Investor's Business Daily* editorial as to how donations collapsed after Hillary lost the 2016 election to Donald Trump. Her office was for sale; Biden's office was for sale. Again, this is not some pro-Republican screed. Many establishment Republican politicians were, likely, bought and paid for too, swamp creatures in other words. It was awfully strange how many Republican members of the House decided not to run for re-election in 2018,[13] thus throwing the House to the Democrats. Lobbyist dollars are equal opportunity corrupters when it comes to legislation. It took someone, Donald John Trump to be precise, willing to stand up and say, in effect, that "this ends now." He may have chosen other words, but you get the drift.

---

[13] We are not casting aspersions on any members in particular, for surely some had perfectly innocent reasons for stepping down.

"Lock Her Up!" . . . and Him and
Him and Her and Her . . .

Honestly, she should be locked up.[14]

*Hillary Clinton: "It's just awfully good that some-
one with the temperament of Donald Trump is
not in charge of the law in our country."
Donald Trump: "Because you'd be in jail."*[15]

The corruption of our government is not limited to politicians and their families enriching themselves while supposedly "serving" their country. No, the corruption in DC had spread under the Obama and Clinton administrations, cancer-like, to the leading law enforcement and intelligence agencies in the land. Donald Trump called out this corruption and criminality as well.

In what was one of the most stunning moments in American political history—at least in the lifetime of anyone living today—Donald Trump uttered those words, "Because you'd be in jail," to his opponent Hillary Clinton during a nationally televised debate watched by millions. What many neutral observers and opponents of Trump viewed as either another example of his lowbrow, classless humor or the type of threat to jail one's political opponent on trumped up charges which we Americans normally associate with tinpot

---

[14]   Transcript of "Speech that made Trump President," Trollitics, video, 5:37, November 9, 2016, https://www.youtube.com/watch?v=szaKnOhJbow&t=.

[15]   "Presidential Debate – DT: Bc you'd be in jail! – Hillary Clinton vs. Donald Trump," video, 00:36, October 9, 2016, https://www.youtube.com/watch?v=Hbh2qXBMjuY.

dictators of third world countries was, in reality, neither. In the mind of Donald Trump, he was, quite simply, revealing the emperor's nakedness; he was telling the truth. Trump was serious, deadly so.

Everything about his behavior then and since indicates he was sincere. He was telling the truth, and judging from the crowd's reaction, he was not alone. Trump had said, as he did the entire campaign, that which could not be said.

Trump, along with many Americans at the time and quite likely many more since, believed that Mrs. Clinton was part of a corrupt Washington establishment that had broken laws of the United States and gotten away with it on more than one occasion. Previously dismissed by mainstream media outlets as the fevered imaginings of some—to use Clinton's words from the past regarding opponents of her husband—"vast right-wing conspiracy," events during the 2016 campaign and since have put the lie to that notion. Oh, don't misunderstand us. The mainstream media continues to try and dismiss the allegations, but it is more difficult to do that when so much evidence has been revealed.

*

The Clinton Email Scandal

Specifically, Trump was quite likely referring to the Clinton email server scandal, the details of which have been revealed through the first inspector general's report (not the more recent one dealing with Spygate) and which, before that report dropped, were neatly summarized by a series of five videos produced by journalist John Spiropolous, which feature key testimony by Comey before a House Oversight Committee.[16] You should watch them all.

At the heart of the Clinton email scandal lies the undisputed fact that she had a private server set up at her home in Chappaqua, New York, (later moved to a New Jersey location) that she used for government business, including communications which were classified. That act alone, in and of itself, is illegal, a crime. She knew the rules against doing so, or at least should have, as she was briefed on them and had been in and around government for, well, a long time. Simple common sense would dictate that she would know such a set-up was ill-advised and illegal. Later, FBI director James Comey would say that "no reasonable prosecutor" would bring charges against Clinton for her actions concerning the illegal server. He had it wrong. The truth is that no reasonable person with Clinton's experience would fail to know that such a set-up was ill-advised and illegal, and, contra Comey, no reasonable prosecutor would fail to bring charges against most anyone else who engaged in such behavior, which kind of gets to the heart of the question: special treatment and unequal treatment under the law.

Partisans of Mrs. Clinton can try to minimize the importance of such a transgression, perhaps using a species of Hillary's infamous after-the-fact dismissal of questions about the reasons for the Benghazi disaster: "At this point, what difference does it make?" But they are wrong; they are probably

---

[16]   You can watch the first video of the series here: "Clinton Server Scandal_Segment 1," video, 13:57, May 2, 2018, https://www.youtube.com/watch?v=Ikrxv89_2QQ. Once you watch that one, the next four should follow or be easily found.

lying, as one suspects they know the truth deep down, but at the very least, they are wrong. *Do we have a crime yet?*

As the video shows, she denied in testimony that government secrets were involved, claiming that there was no classified material transmitted. In his own later testimony, James Comey said there was, in fact, such information, some of it with the highest classification possible. Somebody is lying. *Do we have a crime yet?*

Specifically, Comey said in his testimony that 110 emails in 52 chains were "determined to contain classified information at the time." He gave further details: 8 were top secret, 36 secret at the time, and 8 confidential. Many more were upgraded to classified, "about 2000." When these facts came out, the woman whom many thought should be our president changed her story, asserting that none were "marked" classified. Comey himself noted that that was not true but that even if certain documents are not marked classified, individuals with that level of security clearance are still obligated to know what is and is not classified and to protect the information. *Do we have a crime yet?*

In a well-remembered moment from the campaign of 2016, Comey, on national television, announced that Clinton would not be charged. But he did so in the strangest way possible. For one thing, for the FBI director to call such a press conference to make the announcement was unusual in and of itself. And for another, as everyone likely remembers, he essentially outlined the case for the prosecution and said there was evidence (presumably of "chargeable" behavior) but that, although there was evidence, it was their judgment (begs the question who "they" are) that, in one of the lines for which he will be remembered in history, "no reasonable prosecutor would bring such a case."

Comey was wrong when he said that no reasonable prosecutor would bring such a case, as later revelations would make clear. Trump was right when he would chant along with his fans, "Lock her up!" Granted, many of his supporters were perhaps driven by nothing so much as long-harbored animus against Mrs. Clinton and her husband. But the stark truth is that the average American at the time had no idea how bad things truly were.

The Fix Was In

The entire investigation into the Hillary Clinton private server email scandal was a fraud. From beginning to end, the ultimate result was a foregone conclusion. The only question for the corrupt individuals directing it was how to get there.

Among the evidence for that assertion is the fact that Comey had drafted his "speech" exonerating Clinton months before, two months before in fact, sharing it with others on May 2. This was even before numerous significant witnesses were interviewed. Once other members of the FBI's leadership, including Andrew McCabe, saw Comey's draft, the language describing her actions was changed from Comey's original "grossly negligent," which are the very words used in the statute identifying such behavior as a crime, to "extremely careless." Why was that done? Common sense tells us that it was done to better sweep the entire affair under the rug.

Perhaps the most impassioned questioning of James Comey on the subject of the private server was done by

Will Hurd (R-TX). A former CIA undercover agent himself, Hurd knows the importance of protecting classified information, sources, and methods. Asked by Hurd why no charges were brought, Comey said that two things need to be present: mishandling and criminal intent.

In saying so, James Comey, director of the FBI, misrepresented the truth. Intent has nothing to do with it in these matters. Hurd, incredulous at what he was hearing, asked if not bringing charges was the unanimous opinion among those on the case. Comey said it was so among "the team of agents, investigators, analysts, technologists, yes." Such an assertion again begs the question: who made up the team, at least the team that ultimately decided? That is an interesting question, and what is even more interesting is the fact that the "team" that by and large protected Mrs. Clinton would turn out to have some of the same players that later tried to take down President Trump with the Russia hoax, a group which certainly has lived up to the old coach's cliché about the word "team" standing for "Total Effort Amongst Many." These characters certainly gave their all both to protect Hillary and to destroy Donald.

Other astonishing facts about the mishandling of the investigation by "the team" came out during Comey's testimony. In the video, Tom Marino (R-PA) asked him, one former prosecutor to another, why no grand jury was impaneled as, in his experience, that is the best way to gather evidence and, when needed, compel testimony, with the threat of being held in contempt and going to jail serving as "encouragement" to the witnesses to be forthcoming. Why was not standard prosecutorial practice followed in this investigation?

Failure to call a grand jury was far from the only irregularity in this cover-up, however. Cheryl Mills and Heather Samuelson, Hillary's lawyers and potential witnesses for crying out loud, sat in on her interview with members of "the team." As John Ratcliffe (R-TX) noted, allowing central witnesses in a case to sit in on the interview of the subject of a criminal investigation never happens. Not even on TV. Occam's razor tells us the fix was in.

Missing Evidence

Any good cover-up needs evidence to be covered up, and in this sordid affair of Hillary Clinton's private server, there was no shortage of potential evidence that went missing. For us Catholics, the list reads like a litany of criminality:

- original apple server: missing
- laptops: missing
- thumb drive: missing
- blackberries with sim cards: missing
- thirteen mobile devices lost, discarded or destroyed with a hammer (You read that right.)
- two iPads: missing
- various server backups: missing
- copies of emails from Clinton to Mills and Samuelson: missing (Not only were they missing, they had been wiped clean with BleachBit *after they were subpoenaed.*) As an aside, Congressman Trey Gowdy was quoted as saying, "She and her lawyers had those emails deleted. And they didn't just push the delete

button; they had them deleted where even God can't read them. . . . They were using something called BleachBit. You don't use BleachBit for yoga emails or bridemaids emails. When you're using BleachBit, it is something you really do not want the world to see."[17]

- email archive from Platte River network: missing (It had been deleted.)
- backups of server: missing (They had also been deleted.)

As John Ratcliffe (R-TX) said at the time, "Anyone of those . . . says obstruction of justice. Collectively, they scream obstruction of justice."

This list of missing evidence leads those with eyes to see and ears to hear to certain conclusions. But, first, let us consider a fundamental question. Why should one not set up a private server for government business in their basement? And, conversely, why would one be tempted to do so?

Federal government work email belongs to the federal government and should be conducted on a .gov account. We can surmise that this is so in order to protect the security of said communications, keep things "above board"—i.e., discourage corruption—and also to more easily preserve records and make them easy to find, both for historical purposes and also to be responsive to Freedom of Information Act (FOIA) requests. FOIA requests are a fundamental tool by which the American people keep our government honest.

---

[17] Louis Nelson, "Gowdy: Clinton used special tool to wipe email server," Politico, August 25, 2016, https://www.politico.com/story/2016/08/hillary-clinton-emails-bleachbit-227425.

A certain left of center newspaper has taken as its slogan the saying "Democracy dies in darkness." They are right, though one may argue that they themselves have tried to turn out the lights or at least control the dimmer.

Be that as it may, democracy does die in darkness, and corruption thrives. We Catholics should be concerned with integrity and honesty, or the lack thereof, in government whatever our party affiliation. That is what this aspect of our look at Trump is about. Many of his enemies have accused him of almost every crime under the sun. Some of us intuited something early on, while others only recently are beginning to realize the stunning fact: there is no evidence whatsoever that Donald Trump is guilty of the various accusations lodged against him. None. Well, he is crude at times. The recent sham impeachment made this fact even more clear; the Democrats, in their own articles drafted to impeach the man, mentioned not a single crime.

On the other hand, there is overwhelming evidence that Hillary Clinton and her team committed a crime by setting up a private server and then sought to destroy evidence, again a crime, to cover it up (to say nothing of other crimes associated with the Clinton Foundation and Spygate). Who was involved in the effort to destroy evidence? And, ask yourself, do you honestly believe that if Donald Trump had not won the election, we would know as much of this as we do?

***

The above paragraphs describe the crime; the following will describe a few aspects of the cover-up.

We need not go into all the details. Rather, our interest

lies in the humorous—were it not so serious—account of the efforts of one Platte River employee in particular to aid in the cover up, knowingly or unknowingly. The House Select Committee on Benghazi was established in May of 2014. In July of that year, it struck an agreement with the State Department to produce certain records for the committee. Right around that time—funny that—Clinton attorney Cheryl Mills and Bryan Pagliano, the State Department employee then in charge of the private server, asked the technician in charge of the Clinton account at Platte River, a man named Paul Combetta, if there was a way to hide Hillary's email address from her communications. Combetta went on the internet to a site called Reddit to find out how to do as they requested.

This episode all came to light again during Comey's appearance before the House Judiciary Committee.[18] Congressman Jim Jordan (R-OH), in his questioning of Comey, put Combetta's Reddit inquiries on the big screen. Jordan quoted: "I need to strip out a VIP's (very VIP) email address from a bunch of archived email. Basically they don't want the VIP address exposed to anyone." Jordan rightly asked Comey to whom "they" and "VIP" referred. He specifically asked if it was likely that the VIP was Clinton, to which Comey replied, "Yes." Jordan asked if it was likely that the "they" of Combetta's Reddit query would be Mills or other members of Clinton's staff. Comey said he did not know.

Anyway, Combetta found out via the Reddit community that, unfortunately, he could not "strip out" the email

---

18   You can see Jordan grilling Comey here: https://www.youtube.com/watch?v=r5PJwGLMrLo.

address of the very important person in question. His Reddit questions lay there obscurely online for two more years until just a week before Comey made his appearance before Jordan and the rest of the House Judiciary Committee, at which point Combetta sprang into action again and returned to Reddit to try to delete them. Jim Jordan made a most natural assumption and said, "Director, when I hear 'strip out email address,' sounds like a cover up." *Do we have a crime yet?*

But that is not all. You may remember (many of you may not) Mr. Combetta and his famous "Oh, sh*t" moment. "Oh, sh*t" is right! In December of 2014, Mills, et al, finished sorting through Clinton's emails and sent roughly thirty thousand of them to the State Department as requested. But these were only those which Mills, Samuelson, and their team were allowed to decide were work emails; thousands of others were claimed to be personal and deleted. Because a copy of all email remains on the server at Platte River, Mills told Combetta to erase all duplicates, but he forgot to do so . . . until, that is, the emails got subpoenaed by the Benghazi committee. Combetta told the FBI that was his "'Oh, sh*t,' moment." Then it was that another term entered the American political lexicon: BleachBit, a technological tool used by Clinton's people in a desperate gambit to erase that which should not be seen.

Motive

The whole l'affaire Combetta gets to motive. Motive, on the part of Hillary Clinton and her circle, to conceal select emails from rightful governmental and public oversight. The effort to conceal was an effort to hide her emails—not all of them mind you, just the ones they wanted to—from congress, reporters, and FOIA requests. It was an effort to hide something because, well, she had something to hide. That was the purpose of the private server. That there would be no official records for certain governmental business emails by the secretary of state should be stunning to anyone not blinded by prejudice. The potential for corruption, criminality, and malfeasance when there is no official "paper" or electronic trail should also be obvious. Clinton denied that such obstruction of public accountability and oversight was her motive, and she claimed the private server was authorized. But even that claim was revealed to have been untruthful by Inspector General Steve Linick, as seen in the fifth video in Spiropolous's series. *Do we have a crime yet?*

We could go on, but this probably shows that something was terribly wrong in terms of corruption and criminality in the administrations prior to that of Donald Trump. Many people were put off by and so dismissed candidate Trump's claims about the corrupt establishment, as he brusquely and aggressively called out both financial corruption and the corruption involved in protecting officials from prosecution. But with the passage of time, he has been proven right. One would think that these stories would have been chased down by those media outlets with the most resources and the most reach. One would be wrong. For this is the era of "Fake News."

4

FAKE NEWS

The information provided by the media is at the service
of the common good. Society has a right to information
based on truth, freedom, justice, and solidarity.

Catechism of the Catholic Church 2494

Let's be clear on one thing: the corporate media in our country is no
longer involved in journalism. They're a political special interest no
different than any lobbyist or other financial entity with a total po-
litical agenda, and the agenda is not for you; it's for themselves. Any-
one who challenges their control is deemed a sexist, a racist, a xeno-
phobe, and morally deformed. They will lie, lie, lie, and then again,
they will do worse than that. They will do whatever's necessary."[1]

IF the ensuing years since his election have demonstrated anything, it is the mainstream media's wholesale commitment
to Donald Trump's destruction rather than honest efforts to
cover the news and hold public officials accountable. The
two main channels considered—actually blatantly, but let's
say considered—anti-Trump, CNN and MSNBC, have
given short shrift to his many accomplishments enumerated

---

[1]   Transcript of "Speech that made Trump President," Trollitics,
       video, 5:37, November 9, 2016, https://www.youtube.com/
       watch?v=szaKnOhJbow&t=.

in appendix 2. Rather, they have demonstrated a remarkably single-minded focus on anything and everything, no matter how thinly sourced or dubious, that would reflect poorly on the man and tend to his undoing. Examples abound, and those people reading this book who favor those two networks know it is true. How many pro-Trump pieces have you seen over the past three years, or, forget about pro-Trump, how many objective news reports on his accomplishments have you seen?

Not too many we would be willing to bet. Rather, you have been fed a steady diet of the following stories, and others like them, that the "fake news" pushed until they were proven wrong.

- The Mueller investigation and report; the results of which they did not like. No collusion, no obstruction; it gave Donald Trump a clean bill of health. The aforementioned media outlets, along with many others, devoted a huge percentage of their coverage during the Mueller investigation to their expected outcome. Seemingly on a weekly basis, we were treated to some new "bombshell" that indicated that Mueller was going to take down the president; in the eyes, ears, and mouths of the anti-Trump media, it was only a matter of time. **They were wrong.**

- The imminent threat of WWIII in the wake of the killing of Quassem Soleimani in Iraq. That never came about; in fact, Trump's leadership seems to have the potential there to reset the Middle East in a way that would usher in a period of relative calm after the disastrous years of Obama, the Clintons, and yes, the Bushes. **They, the fake news, were wrong.**

- The various women that were going to bring down the president: all fizzles, every last one. Nothing there? Where are they now? **Again, they were wrong.**

- The anti-Trump media gave and continues to give a prominent platform to individuals who, for whatever reason, have something negative to say about Donald Trump. Individuals such as Michael Cohen (who is now in jail), Michael Avenatti (in jail), and Lev Parnas (under indictment).

Did these last three guys bring the president down as the anti-Trump media so desperately predicted and hoped? Did any of the other stories? If wishing could make it so, they certainly would have. But they didn't. Again and again, **the fake news was wrong.** Although this book hearkens back to the children's classic "The Emperor's New Clothes," this chapter on the media also calls to mind another one: "The Boy Who Cried Wolf."

In all of the above cases, the "fake news," as Trump dubbed them, more than lived up to that moniker. They were consistently wrong because they have abandoned the practice of journalism, and so, just like the boy in the story, fewer and fewer people believe them. Like Trump or hate him, his indictment of the media has proven to be spot on.

Do Rachel Maddow, Don Lemon, and others like them not realize how ridiculous they look in their desperation to "get" Trump? Or maybe they are finally starting to get it. Just recently, the clip of Don Lemon, anti-Trump political advisor Rick Wilson, and another fellow laughing about and mocking Trump supporters has been making the rounds and has already been turned into a Trump campaign commercial. Hillary Clinton donated the term "deplorables" to his campaign last time around. It is nice of these three super cool characters to contribute to the cause this time around.

Even some in the media who are no fans of the president have taken such "journalists" to task for abandoning professional practices in the mad rush to take down the president. Matt Taibbi, a writer with whom practicing Catholics would disagree on many issues, wrote about precisely this "bombshells-that-never-went-off, egg-on-the-face-inviting" style of reporting in his January 2020 article in *Rolling Stone* magazine entitled "2019: A Year the News Media Would Rather Forget." There, he wrote:

> As a result, countless tales pitched as "bombshells" – often pegged to anonymous sources promising to produce proof later on – have turned into super-errors in hindsight.
>
> Reports by Special Counsel Robert Mueller and Justice Inspector General Michael Horowitz exploded claims that Trump lawyer Michael Cohen had met with Russian hackers in Prague, that probable cause existed to believe Trump aide Carter Page was a foreign agent, that Russia and Trump were communicating via a secret Internet server, that evidence existed of Russian efforts to sexually blackmail Trump, that

Russians had vetoed Mitt Romney as Secretary of State, and many others.

Other bombshells . . . died on the launch pad.[2]

As these words are being written, the House impeachment managers are trotting out the Russia collusion nonsense as if the Mueller Report never happened. These people are rather scary "true believers."

Anyone that hopes to consume news in a rational way must be aware of certain things: chief among them the perspective, or editorial slant, or bias of the producer of any particular news item. We don't think we need to list the major ones here as most people are probably aware of their respective biases. That said, a new phenomenon is noticeable with the advent of the presidency of Donald Trump.

A viciousness and single-mindedness of purpose in destroying the man and his presidency is easily discernible. Nobody can deny that Trump has achieved much, or at the very least done things in terms of policy, that would normally be considered praiseworthy, to say nothing of "newsworthy." But, more often than not, channels such as CNN or MSNBC, during this first term of his presidency, have been far more likely to run stories on the Mueller probe, or exposés of Trump's alleged infidelities from the past, or stories of how he is racist, or sexist, or a fledgling Hitler, rather than any mention, let alone focus, on the remarkable gains in the stock market, foreign policy breakthroughs,

---

[2]   Matt Taibbi, "2019: A Year the News Media Would Rather Forget," *Rolling Stone*, January 2, 2020, https://www.rollingstone.com/politics/political-commentary/taibbi-2019-news-media-932789/.

employment numbers, details of the highly successful trade deals negotiated, hostages returned, et cetera. And it would be too much to ask, of course, for any positive reporting on what Trump has accomplished for the pro-life cause, for that constitutes an assault on personal freedom in the minds of the media elite. As an aside, John had the "pleasure" of watching *Morning Joe* this morning while flipping channels. Within a couple of minutes, he was treated to the host, Joe Scarborough, referencing Stalin. "Just on time," he thought, as he changed the channel.

The term "Trump derangement syndrome" has been coined to describe people who hate the man so much that all perspective is lost. We Catholics know that wrath is one of the seven deadly or capital sins, those sins from which so many others flow. In the case of the media, their hatred for Donald Trump has led to a true doubling and tripling down on fake news—that is, lying.

The level of hatred directed at President Trump is unlike anything else we have seen in the last century. Yes, politics has been a blood sport for some time, and conservatives missed no opportunity to attack Clinton and then Obama. Undoubtedly, there is a certain level of hatred on that side. But the Trump case is truly special and is more often than not based on false witness, lies, and slanders, sins enumerated in the *Catechism*, designed to destroy the man and his family.

The following constant fake news themes are just some of the accusations that qualify as such.

Trump is racist. No, he is not. Nothing from the man's past or present life supports such a charge. He has long been friends with people of all cultures and ethnicities. Look at the rapport he has quickly developed with foreign leaders from countries as diverse as China, Saudi Arabia, Egypt, Italy, Japan, and even North Korea. As the mainstream media lobbed these unfounded accusations at the man, the silent majority looked on and considered the Donald Trump they have seen on TV and in the news for the last few decades and thought, "Fake news!"

Perhaps the most vivid demonstration of the media's biased attempts to paint him as a racist centered around the Charlottesville tragedy, after which the lie that he supported white supremacists dominated the headlines. An article by Steve Cortes explains that Trump actually said:

> "Excuse me, they didn't put themselves down as neo-Nazis, and you had some very bad people in that group. But you also had people that were very fine people on both sides. You had people in that group – excuse me, excuse me, I saw the same pictures you did. You had people in that group that were there to protest the taking down of, to them, a very, very important statue and the renaming of a park from Robert E. Lee to another name."

After another question at that press conference, Trump became even more explicit:

> **"I'm not talking about the neo-Nazis and white nationalists because they should be condemned totally."**[3]

3   Steve Cortes, "Trump Didn't Call Neo-Nazis 'Fine People.' Here's Proof." *RealClear Politics*, March 21, 2019, https://www.realclear politics.com/articles/2019/03/21/trump_didnt_call_neo-nazis_fine_people_heres_proof_139815.html.

Cortes goes on to describe how, even in the face of that clear disavowal of white supremacists, the lie that "Trump's a racist" became the narrative. Look up old clips of him with Jesse Jackson, Oprah Winfrey, and other prominent black Americans, even Don King. They did not consider him to be a racist. Donald Trump was never called a racist until he ran for and won the office of president of the United States. That tells you something. As Cortes wrote, "For any honest person, therefore, to conclude that the president somehow praised the very people he actually derided, reveals a blatant and blinding level of bias."

As this is being written, Trump is gaining more and more momentum with voters of every race. Consult his accomplishments for the black community in the list in the appendix. Consider his efforts on behalf of Historically Black Colleges and Universities (HBCUs) and to rid Latino communities of MS-13, his outreach to Native Americans and Asian Americans and ask yourself what right Don Lemon and others have to call this man racist. The accusation is a lie, a slander which the anti-Trump media repeats in the hopes of proving the truth of the "big lie" strategy attributed to Nazi Joseph Goebbels: "If you tell a lie big enough and keep repeating it, people will eventually come to believe it."[4]

Happily, their strategy is failing for it is so obviously untrue. That they keep repeating it is a testament to their dishonesty.

Trump is a misogynist and a rapist and a sexist and an

---

[4]   "Joseph Goebbels: On the 'Big Lie,'" Jewish Virtual Library, accessed March 3, 2020, https://www.jewishvirtuallibrary.org/joseph -goebbels-on-the-quot-big-lie-quot.

all-around bad guy when it comes to women. No, he is not. He seems to have been a playboy and, perhaps at times in the past, an unfaithful husband more than anything else, if that. But we, the authors, don't even know about that—that is, what he did years ago. We have not researched the New York tabloids from last century and are not sure what we would believe if we did. Crude when among men, sure. A millionaire (or did it start with a *b* even back then?) in New York City in the 1970s and '80s. There is an old saying: "Where there is smoke, there is fire." But the smoke has to be real, not artificially generated. Trump, a non-drinking man-about-town in the public eye for decades, still stands because amidst the media generated "smoke" about sexual assault, there seems to be *nothing* there. Affairs many years ago? Perhaps, but we don't even know that, and we were not voting for president of the parish council. We were voting for president of the United States in 2016 and are preparing to do so again in 2020. Would we have voted for the Donald Trump of the New York "scene" thirty years ago? We doubt it. But he seems to be very happily married now; his children reflect very well on him. As Catholics, our support for Donald Trump means neither that we think he is without sin—though most of the negative things that have been said and written about him for the last few years are false—nor that we should have to defend every one of his actions. And, yes, what is more, as Catholics, we will leave the lies, slander, and detraction to others.

Trump colluded with Russia. No, he did not. Though this will be covered in greater detail in a different chapter, the entire Russian narrative was a fraud perpetrated on the

American people. As Trump calls it, "a hoax." Even the assertions that we "know" Russia tried to meddle in our election
are largely unproven. We know we are going against many
Trump supporters, or at least appointees, in government
with this opinion, but one cannot or should not so easily
equate the type of Tom and Jerry antics that were uncovered nor associate the activity of some nebulous Russians
with the Russian state. Most likely, Russia carries out intelligence activities like any other great power and attempts to
exert influence in one way or another, but to believe that
there was anything special or out of the ordinary about their
efforts—that is, those of the Russian government—in the
2016 election is, quite simply, not supported by the facts.
The Mueller report, which was supposedly going to find a
"smoking gun," found nothing related to Trump colluding
with Russians. Rather, it cleared him and his campaign of
any and all charges, CNN and MSNBC's hysterical and
constant protestations notwithstanding.

The Fonzi-like inability of the leftist media to be intro-
spective, let alone acknowledge their errors, in the wake of
the Russian hoax blowing up in their faces is disturbing to
watch. Another liberal outlet, *Vox*, has a very interesting article online. In it, Sean Illing interviews the aforementioned
writer Matt Taibbi. It is fascinating to read, as Illing seems
to be at pains to concede some points that Taibbi makes
about the media's failures in promoting the Russia collusion
story but wants to hold onto the notion that much good was
done. Taibbi ain't buying it and pushes back. Here is Taibbi
talking about the mainstream media's reaction to Trump's
election:

Then when he became president, the instantaneous decision was to declare him illegitimate and foreign-aided. . . . But that's not what the press is supposed to do. That's not our job.

Given the seriousness of all this, given the fact that there was this idea floating around in the mainstream that Trump was literally a spy, we absolutely had a responsibility to go down that alley and check it out, but we also had to think about the other possibility, which is, what if it's untrue? Well, if it's untrue, where the hell is this coming from and why? And what was the purpose and what was the motive of the people who wanted us to think this? And we completely abdicated our responsibility in terms of the second half of that equation.[5]

Here Taibbi, again a man of the Left and no friend of President Trump, stands up for the role of an honest and free press. He asked the questions which, in the wake of the Mueller and two Horowitz reports, every honest reporter should be chasing down the answers to: *Well, if it's untrue* (i.e., the claim that Trump was colluding with Russia), *where the hell is this coming from and why? And what was the purpose and what was the motive of the people who wanted us to think this?*

There is a meme from an HBO series called *True Detective*.

5   Sean Illing, "Did the media botch the Russia story? A conversation with Matt Taibbi." *Vox*, April 1, 2019, https://www.vox.com/2019/3/31/18286902/trump-mueller-report-russia-matt-taibbi.

It is apparently a crime show of some sort; we've not seen it. But in the meme, actor Matthew McGonaughey is pictured; he looks tough, he looks menacing, sitting there drinking from a flask and smoking a cigarette as he tells the detectives interviewing him, "Start asking the right f-ing questions." That is what we need our media to do; that is what we need our law enforcement to do; that is what we as Catholics need to do. Hold the f-word if you like, but if the mainstream media were not fake news, they would be asking these questions and more. And Trump's nickname for the mainstream media would not resonate with the American public so well if they began doing so.

The Church's Views on the Role of the Media

In the *Catechism of the Catholic Church*, we find the Church's teaching on the media and its responsibilities included under the eighth commandment: "You shall not bear false witness against your neighbor." Serious stuff apparently. "The information provided by the media is at the service of the common good. Society has a right to information based on truth, freedom, justice, and solidarity: 'The proper exercise of this right demands that the content of the communication be true and — within the limits set by justice and charity — complete. Further, it should be communicated honestly and properly. This means that in the gathering and in the publication of news, the moral law and the legitimate rights and dignity of man should be upheld.'"[6]

---

[6]   CCC 2494.

Communicated honestly and properly. Traditionally, media stories required solid sourcing. In the Trump era, we have been treated to one of the most prolific sources in American journalism history: "an anonymous source close to . . ." This person who is seemingly everywhere and nowhere has been cited so frequently in anti-Trump stories we are surprised he, or she, does not have a daytime talk show. Trump's administration has been plagued by hostile "leaks" to the media on an unprecedented scale.

As an aside, those who pay close attention have heard the president say or tweet on more than one occasion, "The leaks are real, the news is fake." Trump, knowing that those in government who oppose him (i.e., the resistance) use media leaks (a felony in many instances) as a political weapon, entered office with a plan to counter that collusive abuse between Obama administration hold-overs and their media contacts. He is prudent after all. When Trump tells us that the leaks are real but the news is fake, he is telling all the world with eyes to see and ears to hear that he has set traps for leakers and their media accomplices, traps into which they have been all too willing to fall. Some media figures, as well as their illicit sources in government, have already been exposed in this way, and more are sure to come. Watch the future news, and we will see if we are proven correct on that score.

The record of the media with regards to this search and concern for truth, their most basic function, has been abysmal. Exhibit A could be its longstanding ignoring of the hundreds of thousands of pro-lifers who have marched on Washington, DC, each year for nearly half a century. A massive, massive rally by any measure. And yet, the media has not covered it. True stories that they don't want to push are ignored in favor of narrative engineering efforts and attack pieces on those with whom they disagree.

In the case of the president, no anti-Trump story, no matter how sensationalistic, was too "out there" to run without being properly vetted. The media in this country has needed calling out for many years, and Trump does the country a great service in doing so. You may not like his style, but the way in which he has masterfully used social media to communicate directly with his audience, thereby bypassing the traditional gatekeepers of what the public is allowed to hear, has been remarkably effective and invites a quick discussion of the new media landscape, a landscape which, despite its pitfalls, levels the playing field in a way in which the great Catholic writer of the Edwardian age Hilaire Belloc would applaud.

Again, the *Catechism*: "'It is necessary that all members of society meet the demands of justice and charity in this domain.[7] They should help, through the means of social communication, in the formation and diffusion of sound public opinion.' Solidarity is a consequence of genuine and right communication and the free circulation of ideas that further knowledge and respect for others."[8]

---

[7] The authors concede that Trump is not an exemplar of charitable speech, given his penchant for assigning nicknames to his opponents. But that hardly outweighs the overwhelming reasons for voting for him, and truth be told, we, like most of his supporters, greatly enjoy these humorous jabs. We never claimed to be perfect either.

[8] CCC 2495.

Though the internet is certainly far from an unmixed blessing, in the area of news dissemination and the cultivation of a truly free press, it is a positive good. Before you laugh and dismiss that notion based on the joke "I read it on the internet . . . ," consider the following.

With the advent of the internet, a wide variety of media and access to public files and records is now accessible at the stroke of a keyboard. One can read and digest news from a variety of sources much more easily than ever before. Of course, most people read only news sources that confirm them in their own biases or thoughts. That is a mistake according to Belloc. One of the most prolific writers in the English language, Belloc is known for his historical work, his essays, his humorous prose for children . . . well, he wrote a lot and very well.

The Free Press, first published in 1918 and one of his underappreciated books, is especially germane to this discussion. In it, he identifies a couple of pernicious influences on "the press" of his time, which only now, in our time, have been effectively countered by the advent of the internet: consolidation and the role and incredible power of the advertiser or, in more broad terms, money. Before this consolidation occurred, Belloc describes a landscape in which "one man could print and sell profitably a thousand copies of his version of a piece of news, of his opinions, or those of his clique. There were hundreds of other men who, if they took the pains, had the means to set out a rival account and a rival opinion. We shall see how . . . these safeguards decayed and the bad characters described were increased to their present enormity."[9]

Along with the consolidation, which has proceeded apace and continues today among print newspapers as well as other forms of media, he pointed out the power of money. He specifically called out advertisers, often powerful business interests that the corporate newsmen of his day dared not cross. According to Belloc, the newsman of his day "was compelled to respect his advertisers as his paymasters."[10]

Today, one could consider it less the power solely, or even principally, of the advertisers and more generally the power of special interests, whether business, governmental, well-funded pressure groups such as the LGBTQ movement, or whatever. Those special interests, it seems, now control the advertisers themselves and, for that matter, seem to dictate the censorship and "de-platforming" policies of Big Tech such as Facebook and Twitter.

But the keys to the power of the mass media are money and reach and a uniform ideology, or "groupthink."

With regards to money, in the past there was no widespread challenger to the received opinion of the mainstream media outlets. Of course, there have always been journals and radio shows that went beyond what was "acceptably" right or left, but as a rule, their money was limited and, as a consequence, so was their reach.

Talk radio blew that up somewhat; Rush Limbaugh's massive success drove reach first then money, but the true game-changer has, without a doubt, been the internet.

9   Hilaire Belloc, *The Free Press* (Norfolk: IHS Press, 2002), 31.
10   Ibid., 34.

As long as the mainstream media had a stranglehold on the discourse, their ideology and their narrative went unchallenged. As the majority of university journalism professors now embrace leftist perspectives, many even radical leftist, those views are passed on to their students, who then enter the profession with something less than the desired objectivity perhaps. Even if it were not true that most corporate journalists were men and women of the Left, the consolidation of the press has led to the phenomenon of talking points being disseminated across the ecosystem so that corporate news talking heads parrot one another. Humorous clips have been cobbled together showing dozens of news anchors across the country using the exact same words to tell a story.

Those three factors—money, reach, and uniformity of ideology—gave the media their power and, consequently, a sort of role as "kingmaker" and, for that matter, "-unmaker." "It is the advent of the great newspaper owner as the true governing power in the political machinery of the State, superior to the officials in the State, nominating ministers and dismissing them, imposing policies, and, in general, usurping sovereignty,"[11] was how Belloc phrased it.

This remained the case until Donald Trump came upon the scene and boldly said that the emperor that is the mainstream media has no clothes. The media has been accustomed for many years to framing the narrative, manipulating opinion, and, yes, making and breaking political careers, even promoting wars through their coverage or cover-ups. It has worked well for a long time. Consider the famous quote by

---

[11]   Ibid., 38.

William Randolph Hearst during the run up to the Spanish-American war: "You furnish the pictures and I'll furnish the war." This was in reply to artist Frederic Remington who had been dispatched to Cuba for Hearst's newspaper. Remington had cabled Hearst telling him that there did not look like there would be a war. Hearst's reply revealed an awareness of his power and a willingness to use it to manipulate public opinion in a desired direction. And, yes, of course, there was a war.

But the media's ability to drive policy has been greatly diminished in the age of the internet and social media. Non-mainstream media outlets, the "free press" as Belloc would call them,[12] now have a platform their ancestors would envy. On a more massive scale, President Trump uses the ultimate bully pulpit, his Twitter account, which has more than seventy million followers, to great effect.

Now, at the click of a mouse, a consumer of news can fact check articles, as many are linked to its source documents. A book like this (especially its ebook version), with so many links out to articles and videos, allows for a much more educated consumer of news. We are no longer at the mercy of the narrative engineers of the mainstream media. Their power of monopoly is finally dead; the internet killed it. Donald Trump and his grassroots populist movement have merely presided over the funeral rites and tossed the first shovelful of dirt over the grave.

In terms of the power of the media to personally destroy

---

[12]   But make no mistake, we are not endorsing the views of any or all alternative outlets in particular; you have to use your informed judgment when evaluating them.

someone's career, the fact that it has not worked with Donald Trump is an anomaly, for that power remains. But if it has not worked with Trump, that begs the question, "Why?" For one thing, he must be "clean," an oddity in itself in Washington perhaps. But he is also willing to fight back. He is one of a kind in his capacity to not only be unafraid of the media but to campaign on his absolute disdain and contempt for them, which is much deserved in the opinion of these two Catholics for the reasons enumerated in this chapter. Could any other person have withstood what he did during the campaign of 2016 or in the years since? No. He is one of a kind, and this is yet another reason to vote for the man. He is fearless; he is courageous; he is a warrior, and he will not be cowed.

His willingness (not to be underestimated in comparison with other politicians) and ability to go directly to the people with a bombshell "scoop" in large part mitigates the following observation by Belloc a century ago. "Men gradually came to notice that one thing after another of great public interest, sometimes of vital public interest, was deliberately suppressed in the principal great official papers, and that positive falsehoods were increasingly suggested, or stated."[13]

Remember his tweets in March of 2017 alleging that the Obama administration had "tapped" his phones at Trump Tower? They were widely dismissed and mocked by many, but he was right. Not literally, perhaps, in his use of out of date parlance for spying and surveillance, but essentially, yes, he was right. He put it out there, an idea which once would have been well and easily suppressed by the media

---

[13]   Ibid., 59.

gatekeepers; the essential truth of its claim has been demonstrated right before our eyes over the last few months and years, and there is nothing the "fake news" can do about it. To again borrow the motto of the *Washington Post*, democracy was dying in the darkness, but it was the manipulation and suppression of the news and a politically-motivated refusal to ask the right and obvious questions on the part of the press that was killing it. It is hoped that future journalists will learn lessons from this particularly disgraceful period of journalistic malpractice.

5

THE PEOPLE VERSUS
THE GLOBAL ELITES

*The Magisterium recognizes the importance of national sover-
eignty, understood above all as an expression of the freedom that
must govern relations between States. Sovereignty represents the
subjectivity of a nation, in the political, economic, social and even
cultural sense. The cultural dimension takes on particular importance as a source of strength in resisting acts of aggression or forms
of domination that have repercussions on a country's freedom.
Culture constitutes the guarantee for the preservation of the identity
of a people and expresses and promotes its spiritual sovereignty.[1]*

Compendium of the Social Doctrine of the Church 435

*Our great civilization, here in America and across the civilized
world, has come upon a moment of reckoning. We've seen it in the
United Kingdom, where they voted to liberate themselves from
global government and global trade deals, and global immigration deals that have destroyed their sovereignty and have destroyed
many of those nations. But the central base of world political power*

---

[1]   Pontifical Council for Justice and Peace, *Compendium of the Social
Doctrine of the Church* (Washington, DC: USCCB Publishing,
2005), no. 435, http://www.vatican.va/roman_curia/pontifical_
councils/justpeace/documents/rc_pc_justpeace_doc_20060526_
compendio-dott-soc_en.html#Defending peace.

is right here in America, and it is our corrupt political establish-
ment that is the greatest power behind the efforts at radical glo-
balization and the disenfranchisement of working people. Their
financial resources are virtually unlimited, their political resources
are unlimited, their media resources are unmatched, and most
importantly, the depths of their immorality is absolutely unlimit-
ed. The only thing that can stop this corrupt machine is you. The
only force strong enough to save our country is us. The only people
brave enough to vote out this corrupt establishment is you, the
American people. We are going to have a policy: America first.[2]

IN addition to those many members of the mainstream media who loathe him, Donald Trump has made enemies aplenty, chief among them the "global elite." For he has inspired—or if not inspired, then, through his victory and his speeches given tremendous hope and encouragement to—other populist movements around the world. Consider England and Brexit, the historic vote taken by the British people to leave the EU.[3] That referendum, the result of which was to leave, was taken in 2016. Nearly four years later, they are finally achieving that for which they voted. This is not the first

---

[2]   Transcript of "Speech that made Trump President," Trollitics, video, 5:37, November 9, 2016, https://www.youtube.com/watch?v=szaKnOhJbow&t=.

[3]   Though, in one sense, Trump's victory could be considered to have inspired Brexit, in reality "Brexiteers" have been laboring against the UK's absorption into the European Union for years. Nobody did that more effectively than Nigel Farage in the belly of the beast, at the EU parliament itself. A decade ago, I was often entertained and inspired by Farage's scathing denunciations of the overreach and dictatorial impulses of the global elite in Brussels. You can view a compilation of some of his best speeches here: https://www.youtube.com/watch?v=HhGNoZfvRoA.

instance of the political global elite, who profess "democratic values," attempting to overrule, wait out, or otherwise ignore the will of the people. Their claim to be the great advocates for and protectors of democracy is given the lie always and everywhere when a vote does not go their way. How soon after Trump was elected did "the resistance" begin? And how about their exportation of democracy around the world through the various regime change train wrecks?

Given their track record, it seems to us that the so-called "global elite" are either evil or incompetent. Perhaps both. Their achievements have usually included a new situation in the unlucky countries they go to help in which crony capitalism and corruption are the hallmarks of the governments and economic systems they install . . . for the people who survive their "liberation," at least. So, if Donald Trump uses crude language with such people, well . . .

One can go back to 2008 for a vivid example of the contempt the global elites have both for democracy and for the "Joe Blows" around the world. In that year, the Irish people were presented with a referendum on entry into the EU called the Treaty of Lisbon, which they voted against.

Brendan O'Neil, in an opinion piece in the *Guardian*, wrote:

> Imagine if, following the election of Barack Obama by 52.9% of American voters, the Republican party, which got just 45.7% of votes, demanded another election. Imagine if the Republicans described Obama's victory as a "triumph of ignorance" – brought about by an "unspeakable" and

"ignorant" mass of people who should have been "swatted away by the forces of the establishment" – and insisted on holding a second election so that, this time, the voters could "get it right." . . . EU officials' behind-doors deal to force a second referendum in Ireland reveals their utter contempt for Irish voters, and for democracy itself. It is an historic sucker punch against the sovereignty of the people.[4]

The self-same paragraph could be written about the establishment's reaction to Trump's electoral victory in 2016. The non-coastal elites had spoken, and the establishment, not liking what they heard, set about to undermine his presidency and then to bring him down. Oh, what lovers of "our democracy"—as they so cloyingly call it—they are! Wherever the global elites are challenged throughout the world, they always characterize the regular folks in terms similar to those used in O'Neill's article quoted above.

Globalism—in practice the rule of a base self-appointed/ anointed aristocracy—is a global problem, and happily, in the wake of Trump's victory, anti-globalist parties and politicians have made great strides in returning power to their respective peoples. America First—that is, love of country, home, hearth, and neighbor—has its echoes across the pond in countries such as Poland, Hungary, Slovakia, Austria, and elsewhere. In England, Brexit finally found its champion on

4   Brendan O'Neill, "What part of Ireland's 'no' does the EU not understand?" *The Guardian*, December 13, 2008, https://www. theguardian.com/commentisfree/2008/dec/13/eu-ireland-lisbon -treaty.

Downing Street in Boris Johnson. (It has long had one in the trenches and in the European Parliament in Nigel Farage.) In Italy, Matteo Salvini is once again becoming the chief political power. In Hungary, Viktor Orban is a worthy foil for that arch-villain of globalism George Soros.

Of course, everywhere the populist movement is making progress—that is, the people are asserting themselves over against their political masters—they are slandered by the international fake news media as racists, -phobes of various prefixes, white nationalists, alt-right, and more. But just as was the case in the United States, these accusations are slanders made by those who have much to lose if sovereignty is returned to the people. The authors are Catholic, one of us Mexican-American and the other Irish-American, and we believe racism to be a sin. But we support Donald Trump and the populist movement he leads. You should do the same.

The speech President Trump delivered at the World Economic Forum in Davos, Switzerland on January 21, 2020, was a magnificent thumbing of the nose at the global elites whose construct he has set out to destroy. There he addressed his political enemies, as always displaying the type of courage one does not find among politicians or anyone as a general rule, and told them the many ways in which what he was doing was benefitting his people, and he invited them to do the same for theirs. He was, in fact, quite gracious, as he usually is on the world stage. Will they listen? Who knows? But be assured that their people will hear of this speech.

PRESIDENT TRUMP: Well, thank you very much, Klaus. And a very special congratulations on your 50th year hosting the Annual Meeting of the World Economic Forum. A truly amazing achievement.

It's an honor to address the distinguished members of this organization for the second time as President. When I spoke at this forum two years ago, I told you that we had launched the great American comeback. Today, I'm proud to declare that the United States is in the midst of an economic boom the likes of which the world has never seen before.

We've regained our stride, we discovered our spirit and reawakened the powerful machinery of American enterprise. America is thriving, America is flourishing, and yes, America is winning again like never before.

Just last week alone, the United States concluded two extraordinary trade deals: the agreement with China and the United States-Mexico-Canada Agreement — the two biggest trade deals ever made. They just happened to get done in the same week.

These agreements represent a new model of trade for the 21st century — agreements that are fair, reciprocal, and that prioritize the needs of workers and families. America's economic turnaround has been nothing short of spectacular.

When I took office three years ago, America's economy was in a rather dismal state. Under the previous administration, nearly 200,000 manufacturing jobs had vanished, wages were flat or falling, almost 5 million more Americans had left the labor force than had gotten jobs, and more than 10 million people had been added to the food stamp rolls.

The experts predicted a decade of very, very slow growth

— or even maybe negative growth — high unemployment, and a dwindling workforce, and very much a shrinking middle class. Millions of hardworking, ordinary citizens felt neglected, betrayed, forgotten. They were rapidly losing faith in the system.

Before my presidency began, the outlook for many nations was bleak. Top economists warned of a protracted worldwide recession. The World Bank lowered its projections for global growth to a number that nobody wanted to even think about. Pessimism had taken root deep in the minds of leading thinkers, business leaders, and policymakers.

Yet despite all of the cynics, I had never been more confident in America's future. I knew we were on the verge of a profound economic resurgence, if we did things right — one that would generate a historic wave of investment, wage growth, and job creation.

I knew that if we unleashed the potential of our people, if we cut taxes, slashed regulations — and we did that at a level that's never been done before in the history of our country, in a short period of time — fixed broken trade deals and fully tapped American energy, that prosperity would come thundering back at a record speed. And that is exactly what we did, and that is exactly what happened.

Since my election, America has gained over 7 million jobs — a number unthinkable. I wouldn't say it, I wouldn't talk about it, but that was a number that I had in mind. The projection was 2 million; we did 7 [million] — more than three times the government's own projections.

The unemployment rate is now less than 3, 4, and 5 percent. And at 3.5 percent, that's a number that is the lowest in more than 50 years. The average unemployment rate for my administration is the lowest for any U.S. President in recorded history. We started off with reasonably high rate.

For the first time in decades, we are no longer simply concentrating wealth in the hands of a few. We're concentrating and creating the most inclusive economy ever to exist. We are lifting up Americans of every race, color, religion, and creed.

Unemployment rates among African Americans, Hispanic Americans, and Asian Americans have all reached record lows. African American youth unemployment has reached the lowest it's ever been in the history of our country. African American poverty has plummeted to the lowest rate ever recorded. The unemployment rate for women reached the lowest level since 1953. And women now comprise a majority of the American workforce; that's for the first time.

The unemployment rate for veterans has dropped to a record low. The unemployment rate for disabled Americans has reached an all-time record low. Workers without a high school diploma have achieved the lowest unemployment rate recorded in U.S. history. Wages are rising across the board. And those at the bottom of the income ladder are enjoying the percentage, by far, largest gains.

Workers' wages are now growing faster than management wages. Earnings growth for the bottom 10 percent is outpacing the top 10 percent — something that has not happened. Paychecks for high school graduates are rising faster than for college graduates.

Young Americans just entering the workforce are also sharing in America's extraordinary prosperity. Since I took office, more than 2 million millennials have gotten jobs, and their wages have grown by nearly 5 percent annually — a number that was unthinkable. Nobody would have ever thought it was possible three years ago. A record number of Americans between the ages of 25 and 34 are now working.

In the eight years before I took office, over 300,000 working-age people left the workforce. In just three years in my administration, 3.5 million people have joined the workforce. Ten million people have been lifted off welfare in less than three years. Celebrating the dignity of work is a fundamental pillar of our agenda.

This is a blue-collar boom. Since my election, the net worth of the bottom half of wage earners has increased by plus-47 percent — three times faster than the increase for the top 1 percent. Real median household income is at the highest level ever recorded.

The American Dream is back — bigger, better, and stronger than ever before. No one is benefitting more than America's middle class.

We have created 1.2 million manufacturing and construction jobs — a number also unthinkable. After losing 60,000 factories under the previous two administrations — hard to believe when you hear "60,000 factories" — America has now gained, in a very short period of time, 12,000 new factories under my administration. And the number is going up rapidly. We'll be beating the 60,000 number that we lost, except these will be bigger, newer, and the latest.

Years of economic stagnation have given way to a roaring geyser of opportunity. U.S. stock markets have soared by more than 50 percent since my election, adding more than

$19 trillion to household wealth, and boosting 401(k)s, pensions, and college savings accounts for millions of hard-working families.

And these great numbers are many things, and it's despite the fact that the Fed has raised rates too fast and lowered them too slowly. And even now, as the United States is by far the strongest economic power in the world, it's not even close. It was going to be close, but a lot of good things happened to us, and some not-so-good things happened to certain other places.

They're forced to compete, and we compete with nations that are getting negative rates — something very new — meaning, they get paid to borrow money. Something that I could get used to very quickly. Love that. Got to pay back your loan? Oh, how much am I getting?

Nevertheless, we still have the best numbers that we've had in so many different areas. It's a conservative approach, and we have a tremendous upside potential, when all of the trade deals and the massive deregulation starts kicking in — which will be during this year, especially toward the end of the year. Those trade deals are starting to kick in already. The regulations are kicking in right now.

And I see such tremendous potential for the future. We have not even started, because the numbers we're talking about are massive.

The time for skepticism is over. People are flowing back into our country. Companies are coming back into our country. Many of you, who I know, are coming back in with your plants and your factories. Thank you very much. America's newfound prosperity is undeniable, unprecedented, and unmatched anywhere in the world.

America achieved this stunning turnaround not by making minor changes to a handful of policies, but by adopting a whole new approach centered entirely on the wellbeing of the American worker.

Every decision we make — on taxes, trade, regulation, energy, immigration, education, and more — is focused on improving the lives of everyday Americans. We are determined to create the highest standard of living that anyone can imagine, and right now, that's what we're doing for our workers. The highest in the world. And we're determined to ensure that the working and middle class reap the largest gains.

A nation's highest duty is to its own citizens. Honoring this truth is the only way to build faith and confidence in the market system. Only when governments put their own citizens first will people be fully invested in their national futures. In the United States, we are building an economy that works for everyone, restoring the bonds of love and loyalty that unite citizens and powers nations.

Today, I hold up the American model as an example to the world of a working system of free enterprise that will produce the most benefits for the most people in the 21st century and beyond. A pro-worker, pro-citizen, pro-family agenda demonstrates how a nation can thrive when its communities, its companies, its government, and its people work together for the good of the whole nation.

As part of this new vision, we passed the largest package of tax cuts and reforms in American history. We doubled the child tax credit, benefitting 40 million American families and lifting 650,000 single mothers and their 1 million children out of poverty — and out of poverty quickly.

We passed the first-ever tax credit for employers who provide paid paternal leave for employees earning $72,000 [or] less annually, and passed paid family leave for government employees as a model for the country.

We made childcare much more affordable and reduced or eliminated childcare waitlists all across the nation. Our childcare reforms are supporting working parents and ensuring their children have access to high-quality care and education, all of which they very much deserve.

We lowered our business tax from the highest in the developed world down to one that's not only competitive, but one of the lower taxes.

We created nearly 9,000 Opportunity Zones in distressed communities where capital gains on long-term investments are now taxed at zero, and tremendous wealth is pouring into areas that for a hundred years saw nothing.

The 35 million Americans who live in these areas have already seen their home values rise by more than $22 billion. My administration has also made historic investments in historically black colleges and universities. I saved HBCUs. We saved them. They were going out, and we saved them.

We're removing roadblocks to success and rewarding businesses that invest in workers, families, and communities.

We've also launched the most ambitious campaign in history to reduce job-killing regulations. For every new regulation adopted, we are removing eight old regulations, which will save an average of American households about $3,100 per year. It was going to be, "for every one, we do two," but we were able to lift that to eight, and we think that's going to go quite a bit higher. We still have a way to go.

Today, I urge other nations to follow our example and liberate your citizens from the crushing weight of bureaucracy. With that, you have to run your own countries the way you want.

We're also restoring the constitutional rule of law in America, which is essential to our economy, our liberty, and our future. And that's why we've appointed over 190 federal judges — a record — to interpret the law as written. One hundred and ninety federal judges — think of that — and two Supreme Court judges.

As a result of our efforts, investment is pouring into our country. In the first half of 2019, the United States attracted nearly one-quarter of all foreign direct investment in the world — think of that. Twenty-five percent of all foreign investment all over the world came into the United States, and that number is increasing rapidly.

To every business looking for a place where they are free to invest, build, thrive, innovate, and succeed, there is no better place on Earth than the United States.

As a central part of our commitment to building an inclusive society, we established the National Council for the American Worker. We want every citizen, regardless of age or background, to have the cutting-edge skills to compete and succeed in tomorrow's workplace. This includes critical industries like artificial intelligence, quantum computing, and 5G.

Under Ivanka's leadership — who is with us today

— our Pledge to America's Workers has become a full-blown national movement with over 400 companies committing to provide new job and training opportunities to already very close to 15 million American students and workers. Fifteen million.

America is making sweeping changes to place workers and their families at the center of our national agenda. Perhaps the most transformative change of all is on trade reform, where we're addressing chronic problems that have been ignored, tolerated, or enabled for decades. Our leaders did nothing about what happened to us on trade.

Before I was elected, China's predatory practices were undermining trade for everyone, but no one did anything about it, except allow it to keep getting worse and worse and worse. Under my leadership, America confronted the problem head on.

Under our new phase one agreement — phase two is starting negotiations very shortly — China has agreed to substantially do things that they would not have done: measures to protect intellectual property; stop forced technology transfers; remove trade barriers in agricultural goods and on agricultural goods, where we were treated so badly; open its financial sector totally — that's done — and maintain a stable currency, all backed by very, very strong enforcement.

Our relationship with China, right now, has probably never been better. We went through a very rough patch, but it's never, ever been better. My relationship with President Xi is an extraordinary one. He's for China; I'm for the U.S. But other than that, we love each other.

Additionally, China will spend an additional $200

billion over two years on American services, agriculture, and energy, and manufactured goods. So we'll be taking in an excess of $200 billion; could be closer to $300 billion when it finishes. But these achievements would not have been possible without the implementation of tariffs, which we had to use, and we're using them on others too. And that is why most of our tariffs on China will remain in place during the phase two negotiations. For the most part, the tariffs have been left, and we're being paid billions and billions of dollars a year as a country.

As I mentioned earlier, we ended the NAFTA disaster — one of the worst trade deals ever made; not even close — and replaced it with the incredible new trade deal, the USMCA — that's Mexico and Canada.

In the nearly 25 years after NAFTA, the United States lost 1 in 4 manufacturing jobs, including nearly 1 in 4 vehicle-manufacturing jobs. It was an incentive to leave the country. The NAFTA agreement exemplified the decades-long failures of the international trading system. The agreement shifted wealth to the hands of a few, promoted massive outsourcing, drove down wages, and shuttered plants and factories by the thousands. The plants would leave our country, make the product, sell it into our country. We ended up with no jobs and no taxes; would buy other countries' product. That doesn't happen anymore.

This is the wreckage that I was elected to clean up. It's probably the reason I ran for President, more than any other thing, because I couldn't understand why we were losing all of these jobs to other countries at such a rapid rate. And it got worse and worse, and I think it's probably the primary reason that I ran, but there are other reasons also. And to replace with a new system that puts workers before the special interests. And the special interests will do just fine, but the workers come first.

Our brand-new USMCA is the result of the broadest coalition ever assembled for a trade agreement. Manufacturing, agriculture, and labor all strongly endorsed the deal. And, as you know, it just passed in Congress overwhelmingly. It shows how to solve the 21st century challenge we all face: protecting intellectual property, expanding digital trade, re-shoring lost jobs, and ensuring rising wages and living standards.

The United States has also concluded a great new trade deal with Japan — approximately $40 billion — and completely renegotiated our deal with South Korea. We're also negotiating many other transactions with many other countries. And we look forward to negotiating a tremendous new deal with the United Kingdom. They have a wonderful new Prime Minister and wants very much to make a deal, as they say.

To protect our security and our economy, we are also boldly embracing American energy independence. The United States is now, by far, the number-one producer of oil and natural gas anywhere in the world, by far. It's not even close.

While many European countries struggle with crippling energy costs, the American energy revolution is saving American families $2,500 every year in lowering electric bills and numbers that people said couldn't happen, and also, very importantly, prices at the pump.

We've been so successful that the United States no longer needs to import energy from hostile nations. With an abundance of American natural gas now available, our European allies no longer have to be vulnerable to unfriendly energy suppliers either. We urge our friends in Europe to use America's vast supply and achieve true energy security.

With U.S. companies and researchers leading the way, we are on the threshold of virtually unlimited reserves of energy, including from traditional fuels, LNG, clean coal, next-generation nuclear power, and gas hydrate technologies.

At the same time, I'm proud to report the United States has among the cleanest air and drinking water on Earth — and we're going to keep it that way. And we just came out with a report that, at this moment, it's the cleanest it's been in the last 40 years. We're committed to conserving the majesty of God's creation and the natural beauty of our world.

Today, I'm pleased to announce the United States will join One Trillion Trees Initiative being launched here at the World Economic Forum. One Trillion Trees. (Applause.) And in doing so, we will continue to show strong leadership in restoring, growing, and better managing our trees and our forests.

This is not a time for pessimism; this is a time for optimism. Fear and doubt is not a good thought process because this is a time for tremendous hope and joy and optimism and action.

But to embrace the possibilities of tomorrow, we must reject the perennial prophets of doom and their predictions of the apocalypse. They are the heirs of yesterday's foolish fortune-tellers — and I have them and you have them, and we all have them, and they want to see us do badly, but we don't let that happen. They predicted an overpopulation crisis in the 1960s, mass starvation in the '70s, and an end of oil in the 1990s. These alarmists always demand the same thing: absolute power to dominate, transform, and control every aspect of our lives.

We will never let radical socialists destroy our economy, wreck our country, or eradicate our liberty. America will always be the proud, strong, and unyielding bastion of freedom.

In America, we understand what the pessimists refuse to see: that a growing and vibrant market economy focused on the future lifts the human spirit and excites creativity strong enough to overcome any challenge — any challenge by far.

The great scientific breakthroughs of the 20th century — from penicillin, to high-yield wheat, to modern transportation, and breakthrough vaccines — have lifted living standards and saved billions of lives around the world. And we're continuing to work on things that you'll be hearing about in the near future that, even today, sitting here right now, you wouldn't believe it's possible that we have found the answers. You'll be hearing about it. But we have found answers to things that people said would not be possible — certainly not in a very short period of time.

But the wonders of the last century will pale in comparison to what today's young innovators will achieve because they are doing things that nobody thought even feasible to begin. We continue to embrace technology, not to shun it. When people are free to innovate, millions will live longer, happier, healthier lives.

For three years now, America has shown the world that the path to a prosperous future begins with putting workers first, choosing growth, and freeing entrepreneurs to bring their dreams to life.

For anyone who doubts what is possible in the future, we need only look at the towering achievements of the past. Only a few hundred miles from here are some of the great cities of Europe — teeming centers of commerce and culture. Each of them is full of reminders of what human drive and imagination can achieve.

Centuries ago, at the time of the Renaissance, skilled craftsmen and laborers looked upwards and built the structures that still touch the human heart. To this day, some of the greatest structures in the world have been built hundreds of years ago.

In Italy, the citizens once started construction on what would be a 140-year project, the Duomo of Florence. An incredible, incredible place. While the technology did not yet exist to complete their design, city fathers forged ahead anyway, certain that they would figure it out someday. These citizens of Florence did not accept limits to their high aspirations and so the Great Dome was finally built.

In France, another century-long project continues to hold such a grip on our hearts and our souls that, even 800 years after its construction, when the Cathedral of Notre Dame was engulfed in flames last year — such a sad sight to watch; unbelievable site, especially for those of us that considered it one of the great, great monuments and representing so many different things — the whole world grieved.

[Though] her sanctuary now stands scorched and charred

— and a sight that's hard to believe; when you got used to it, to look at it now, hard to believe. But we know that Notre Dame will be restored — will be restored magnificently. The great bells will once again ring out for all to hear, giving glory to God and filling millions with wonder and awe.

The Cathedrals of Europe teach us to pursue big dreams, daring adventures, and unbridled ambitions. They urge us to consider not only what we build today, but what . . . will endure long after we are gone. They testify to the power of ordinary people to realize extraordinary achievements when united by a grand and noble purpose.

So, together, we must go forward with confidence, determination, and vision. We must not be timid, or meek, or fearful — but instead we must boldly seize the day and embrace the moment. We have so many great leaders in this room — not only business leaders, but leaders of nations — and some are doing such a fantastic job. We work together very closely. We will draw strength from the glories of the past, and we will make greatness our common mission for the future.

Together, we will make our nations stronger, our countries safer, our culture richer, our people freer, and the world more beautiful than ever before.

Above all else, we will forever be loyal to our workers, our citizens, and our families — the men and women who are the backbone of our economies, the heart of our communities, and the soul of our countries. Let us bring light to their lives one by one and empower them to light up the world.

Thank you very much. God bless you. God bless your

countries. And God bless America. Thank you. Thank you very much.[5]

A magnificent inspiring speech. One wonders how many converts he made there in Davos. But that matters less than how many converts are being made among the people. One passage in particular from the speech calls out the way in which the global elites have promoted various "crises du jour" that require the people ceding ever more power to them and their expertise. Consider the following: "We must reject the perennial prophets of doom and their predictions of the apocalypse. They are the heirs of yesterday's foolish fortune-tellers — and I have them and you have them, and we all have them, and they want to see us do badly, but we don't let that happen. They predicted an overpopulation crisis in the 1960s, mass starvation in the '70s, and an end of oil in the 1990s. These alarmists always demand the same thing: absolute power to dominate, transform, and control every aspect of our lives."

The overpopulation fears such "prophets of doom" stoked contributed to the mass abandonment by Catholics in the '60s and '70s of any commitment to live their sexual lives in keeping with the Church's teaching—that is to say, God's law—most specifically with regards to contraception, which paved the way to increased acceptance of abortion. The global elites have been hard at work ever since promoting

---

[5]   Donald Trump, "Remarks by President Trump at the World Economic Forum | Davos, Switzerland," the Whitehouse, January 21, 2020, https://www.whitehouse.gov/briefings-statements/remarks-president-trump-world-economic-forum-davos-switzerland/.

and imposing the contraceptive mentality on countries rich and poor around the world, often tying foreign aid to such acceptance.

The crisis du jour, of course, is climate change. Let the points be debated, but the thing to watch for is the effort by the elite to use such supposed crises (Really? We only have twelve or fourteen years before impending doom! Seriously?) to gain greater and greater control over our lives. We, for our part, are happy that Trump has the gumption to tell them to leave us alone. In other words, he has announced that *this*—that is, the power that special interest left-wing pressure groups have over the daily lives of American citizens—*ends now.*

6

FOREIGN POLICY

Radical Islamic Terrorism

But out of the desert, from the dry places and the dreadful suns, come the cruel children of the lonely God; the real Unitarians who with scimitar in hand have laid waste the world. For it is not well for God to be alone.[1]

G. K. Chesterton

They will allow radical Islamic terrorists to enter our country by the thousands. They will allow the great Trojan horse — and I don't want people looking back in a hundred years and 200 years and have that story be told about us because we were led by inept, incompetent and corrupt people like Barack Obama and like Hillary Clinton. We don't want to be part of that history.[2]

THROUGHOUT his campaign and his presidency, Donald Trump's refreshing, honest, plain-speaking style, unconstrained by political correctness, resonated with ordinary Americans, Catholic and non-Catholic alike, perhaps never

---

[1]   G. K. Chesterton, *Orthodoxy* (Dover Publications, 2004).

[2]   "Speech: Donald Trump – West Palm Beach, FL – October 13, 2016," Factbase Videos, video, 46:36, October 23, 2017, https://youtube/RSw0yMFuPRk.

more than when he dared name "Radical Islamic Terror-ism" as a problem. His predecessor, Barack Obama, often obfuscated the source of much of the suffering around the globe by refusing to name it. And *his* predecessor, Repub-lican George W. Bush, blithely informed us that Islam is a "religion of peace." Bush was wrong; one can hope he was simply misinformed and not consciously lying to the peo-ple.[3] Without question, Islamic terrorism is *the* international challenge to peace.

During the 2016 campaign, Trump got himself into hot water by proposing a halt to Islamic immigration until we figure out "what the hell is going on." Those were the early days of the campaign, and the message was moderated later, but was it so off base? Look at how life in America has changed since September 11. While jihadist-inspired attacks are relatively rare in our country, young people don't remem-ber what it was like to go to the airport or a large sporting event without having to "go through security." In Europe, sadly, jihad-inspired attacks are not so rare, but that is sim-ply a consequence of their much higher levels of Islamic immigration.

Was his prescription off base, or could it be considered simply a temporary exercise of the virtue of prudence? According to the *Catechism*, one of the three essential ele-ments of the common good is "peace, that is the stability and security of a just order. It presupposes that authority

---

[3]   For daily confirmation of this fact, check in on https://thereli gionofpeace.com/ and see the latest atrocities. But be forewarned; much of the reading there is not for the faint of heart. There you will see just how wrong Bush was.

should ensure by morally acceptable means the security of society and its members."[4]

Is it wrong to look at and learn from the experiences of others—countries such as Sweden, France, Germany, and the Netherlands—to see how the lives of their citizens are changing, and not for the better, due to large-scale Islamic immigration? Grooming rape gangs and frequent knife assaults in England, a dramatic spike in violent crime in Sweden, traditionally a very safe society, and "no-go zones" in France? Is that what we want for our children's future?

Is it wrong to consider whether and to what extent certain interpretations of Islam—and perhaps not fringe interpretations but distressingly common ones—are, in fact, incompatible with Western values and American principles?

Is it wrong to feel that perhaps the victims of Islamic terrorism around the world should be given priority as refugees to our country?

Is it wrong to ask any of these questions? No. It is not, but it took a Donald Trump courageously asking these hard but common-sense questions on the national scene—to, in effect, say "the emperor has no clothes"—before more Americans felt comfortable asking them out loud, in public at least.

In the event, no such moratorium was ever enacted. Even Trump's limited "travel ban" subjected him to accusations of xenophobia, racism, and "anti-American" sentiments regarding religious freedom, and had to travel through the courts, where he won, incidentally.

And since the campaign, as president, Trump has

---

[4]   CCC 1909.

solidified alliances with the leaders of Islamic countries who are willing to be genuine partners in the fight against radical Islamic terror. Whereas in Egypt, President Obama and his administration supported the installation of Mohammed Morsi, a member of the Muslim Brotherhood under whom Christians would suffer the same fate as their co-religionists in places like Syria and Iraq, the Trump administration partners closely with the regime of Abdel Fattah el-Sisi, a strongman who will fight the Islamic extremists to the extent he is able. In Libya, the Obama administration, in the person of his secretary of state, Hillary Clinton, gloated that "we came, we saw, he died," a death and "regime change" which cast that country into a maelstrom of misery and jihadist activity and let loose the mass migration of Muslims, many radicals among them no doubt, into Europe, just as Gaddafi warned.

If we are willing to honestly look at our country's foreign policy that led to the rise of ISIS and the attempted genocide and ethnic cleansing of both Christians and Yazidis, what would we learn? How shocked would you be to learn that American foreign policy under the prior administration supported the rise of Islamic radical groups?[5] For what purpose? Does it matter? Does it matter to the poor Middle Eastern Christians in Syria, Iraq, and Lybia?

In dramatic contrast to the prior administration, that of Donald Trump brought the fight to ISIS and began rolling back their caliphate—though truth be told, Russia, allied

---

[5]   One of the most eye-opening accounts of this treachery is a lengthy report compiled by Sundance at Theconservativetreehouse.com called "The Benghazi Brief." Take the time and read it if you are so inclined. You need not do so to continue here, but we consider it vital reading by every American citizen.

with Iranian forces and the Syrian Army of Assad, have done much of the heavy lifting in Syria—whereas under Obama, the black flag rose over ever increasing swathes of territory. Yes, great progress has been made in the fight against radical Islam, a fight that we can trust Donald Trump to lead, but the fight is not over. While many Catholics and other Christians who voted for President Trump because of his anti-neocon, anti-nation building campaign promises would be pleased to see America pull back from those types of interventions, we do have duties towards our suffering brethren around the world, especially those victims of jihad and especially we Catholics to our brothers and sisters in Christ.

With all the news coverage that the Middle East draws, jihad is a global problem, not just a Middle Eastern one. The Gatestone Institute recently published a sobering article about radical Islam's activities in sub-saharan Africa. In it, author Giulio Meotti compares the media coverage of the killing of a pig in China with the lack thereof of the ongoing massacre of Christians in Africa.

> The Bishops' Conference of Nigeria described the area as "killing fields", like the ones the Khmer Rouge created in Cambodia to exterminate the population. Most of the 4,300 Christians killed for their faith during the last year came from Nigeria. Nina Shea, an expert in Religious Freedom, recently wrote: "An ongoing Islamic extremist project to exterminate Christians in sub-Saharan Africa is even more brutal and more consequential for the Church than it is in the Middle East, the

place where Christians suffered ISIS 'genocide', as the U.S. government officially designated."

Unfortunately, the murder of these Christians during the last month has been largely ignored by the Western media. "A slow-motion war is under way in Africa's most populous country. It's a massacre of Christians, massive in scale and horrific in brutality and the world has hardly noticed", wrote the French philosopher, Bernard Henri Lévy.[6]

President Trump, if you ever read this, please consider the plight of those sub-saharan African victims of radical Islam. Read this article by Meotti, and take action, unilateral if necessary, to protect those poor people. We trust that you will not stand idly by but rather endeavor to help them to the extent we are able. We feel no such confidence that any of the Democrat candidates for president in 2020 would take any significant action. Search your own heart and conscience, fellow Catholic readers, as to what you think should be done and who you think would do it.

"These persecuted Christians feel more and more alone in a world that sees them as intruders. They are as if suspended in a limbo, between an amnesic and weak West and a rising radical Islam. There seems to be no way to push the Western world to become aware of this tragedy that no one

---

[6]   Giulio Meotti, "Cruelty to Animals Gets More Media Coverage than Beheaded Christians," Gatestone Institute, January 26, 2020, https://www.gatestoneinstitute.org/15483/animal-cruelty-beheaded-christians.

talks about and which could have fatal consequences for the future of our civilization."[7]

Build the Wall, and Mexico Is Gonna Pay for It

Political authorities, for the sake of the common good for which they are responsible, may make the exercise of the right to immigrate subject to various juridical conditions, especially with regard to the immigrants' duties toward their country of adoption.[8]

Here again, we have a catch phrase of the campaign—"Build that wall!"—which many critics of President Trump assert indicated a virulent racism and animus towards our neighbors to the south. Many Catholics, numerous bishops among them, spoke out strongly against such rhetoric.

The rhetoric was, no doubt, inflammatory, and Trump was and is a flamethrower. But, rhetoric aside, is the reasoning behind such a sentiment not consonant with an informed Catholic worldview? Consider the following passage from the *Catechism*:

> The more prosperous nations are obliged, to the extent they are able, to welcome the foreigner in search of the security and the means of livelihood which he cannot find in his country of origin. Public authorities should see to it that the natural right is respected that places a guest under the protection of those who receive him. Political authorities, for the sake of the common good

---

[7]   Ibid.
[8]   CCC 2241.

for which they are responsible, may make the exercise of the right to immigrate subject to various juridical conditions, especially with regard to the immigrants' duties toward their country of adoption. Immigrants are obliged to respect with gratitude the material and spiritual heritage of the country that receives them, to obey its laws and to assist in carrying civic burdens.[9]

Kevin Clark, writing in *Crisis Magazine* in 2017, commented on the passage in light of the United States Conference of Catholic Bishops' criticism of President Trump on immigration:

> The phrase "to the extent they are able" is obviously a prudential judgment, and as such would need to be exercised by legitimate political authority. The ability of a country to accept immigrants would not be limited by mere physical space, or even by economic opportunities, but also by such issues as the ability to assimilate immigrants in such a way as to maintain peace and social cohesion.
>
> By asserting that "juridical conditions" may be enforced, the *Catechism* further makes it clear that prudential concerns can legitimately limit immigration.
>
> If such issues were not subject to political discernment, and the Church meant to teach that countries can only interdict violent felons, then the *Catechism* would presumably take away the possibility of judgment and merely condemn restrictions on immigration. Yet, it does not do so. By using the language of

---

[9]   CCC 2241.

political judgment and the common good to determine
the number and conditions under which a country
will admit immigrants, the *Catechism* clearly implies
that some would-be immigrants may be excluded.
And if there is a limit to the number of immigrants,
or if some immigrants cannot comply with reasonable
conditions, then a country will need to enforce immigration laws.[10]

Immigration is a complex subject, especially that between
the United States and our near southern neighbor, Mexico.
However, what is not complex or difficult to understand
is that the US-Mexican border served for generations as a
highway for illegal immigration into the United States, and
a most expensive highway at that. A report titled "The Fis-
cal Burden of Illegal Immigration on Taxpayers" cited in
an article in the *Washington Examiner* assessed the cost of
illegal immigration to United States taxpayers at $135 bil-
lion per year.[11] Numbers are thrown around rather breezily
nowadays, but that is billion with a *b*. To paraphrase the old
saying, a few years of $135 billion and pretty soon you'll be
talking real money.

Defenders of uncontrolled immigration—Trump has

10   Kevin Clark, "The USCCB Should Follow the *Catechism* on Im-
      migration," *Crisis Magazine*, September 7, 2017, https://www.
      crisismagazine.com/2017/usccb-follow-catechism-immigration.

11   Paul Bedard, "Record $135 billion a year for illegal immigration,
      average $8,075 each, $25,000 in NY," *Washington Examiner*, Sep-
      tember 27, 2017, https://www.washingtonexaminer.com/record
      -135-billion-a-year-for-illegal-immigration-average-8-075-each
      -25-000-in-ny.

nowhere intimated that he seeks to end legal immigration from Latin America but rather to simply gain control of it—often assert that because America is historically a "nation of immigrants" somehow the country can never seek to slow the numbers coming into the country. That is absurd on many levels. For one thing, earlier waves of immigration did not come into a country with a massive welfare state waiting to receive them and their children. And, for another, before Trump's presidency, the authorities have never taken seriously their task to protect the public by deporting criminals. It is one thing to be in a country illegally but seeking only to make a better life for your family by working hard. It is quite another to commit serious crimes against the native population as well as your own fellow immigrants with impunity and be allowed to remain.

To say that is to invite accusations of racism, or hostility towards the poor, but both charges would be unfair. It would seem to be common sense that massive amounts of immigration combined with a bloated welfare state will place an undue burden on the host country's citizens, as it would be to say that individuals who are in the country illegally who commit violent crimes or are members of criminal organizations should be removed upon apprehension. Again, per the *Catechism*: "Political authorities, for the sake of the common good for which they are responsible, may make the exercise of the right to immigrate subject to various juridical conditions, especially with regard to the immigrants' duties toward their country of adoption. Immigrants are obliged to respect with gratitude the material and spiritual heritage of the country that receives them, to obey its laws and to assist in carrying civic burdens."[12]

The vast majority of immigrants from Mexico and Central America seek nothing so much as a better life. They come here and work hard. However, those two facts do not excuse the representatives of the citizens of the United States from their duty to guard the interests of their constituents.

What Donald Trump has enabled, through his bluntness, is a conversation among adults, one in which easy slanders and charges of the sin of racism have no place. He has allowed us, even those who honestly value much of the heritage of our Catholic neighbors to the south, to admit that our immigration system is broken and needs fixing. What many do not realize is that in so doing, Trump may be the best friend the average Mexican citizen has had in the White House in a long time.

Trump and Obrador: Unlikely Allies?

Mexico recently elected a socialist in Andres Manuel Lopez Obrador. One would think that a man such as that would be a political enemy of Donald J. Trump. But, counterintuitively, since his election, the United States and Mexico have struck a trade deal, the USMCA, to replace NAFTA (North American Free Trade Agreement)—the previous trade agreement between Mexico, the United States, and Canada that was the source of the giant "sucking sound" of jobs leaving

---

[12]   CCC 2241.

the United States referred to by then presidential candidate Ross Perot during his 1992 campaign.

The terms of the new trade deal are expected to greatly benefit many Mexican workers too, with stipulations about their working conditions and pay. Isn't it ironic that Donald Trump, that arch-racist in the twisted minds of the media and so many Democrats, may be responsible for the biggest pay raise in Mexican history?

In some venues, Obrador has even been referred to as the "Mexican Donald Trump." He is called so not for his socialist bona fides but rather for his nationalist ones. Obrador, not unlike Trump, seeks primarily to help the working class of his country. Their approaches may differ, but so far it seems enough commonality has been found to serve as a basis for mutual cooperation and friendly relations.

It is not only on matters of trade that Trump and Obrador have found mutually beneficial common ground; they are cooperating in an unprecedented way on border security too. A good sign is that we now see Mexico deploying its own soldiers at both their northern and southern borders to control immigration both out of and into their own country.

It would be wonderful if a wall was not needed. We are faithful Catholics. One of us is Mexican-American. Both of his parents are from Mexico, and he still has family there, and the other has lived throughout Latin America and has many friends there and a great affection for the people and culture; yet we both think a wall is justified. It would be terrific if everyone respected the immigration laws of a host country and "played by the rules," but they don't. It would be wonderful if the horror stories of coyotes and human trafficking were not real, but they are. It would be wonderful if the Mexican government had provided better living conditions for its people for the past century or so, but it hasn't.

Robert Frost, the great American poet from New England, that land of stone walls, explored the two competing feelings about walls in his famous poem "Mending Wall."

At this point in history, it seems that the tensions between Frost's two expressed ideas—"Something there is that does not love a wall" and "Good fences make good neighbors"—favors the building of a wall. But we may hope that someday, perhaps in the not too distant future, if the new Trump administration trade deal with Mexico bears fruit for the Mexican people, if the threat of cross-border terrorism is eliminated, if the grip of the cartels and human-trafficking over the immigration process is removed . . . if those new conditions come about, the two nations can cooperate in dismantling it.

But for now—given the threat of drugs, the cartels, the direct and indirect cost of illegal immigration to the nation and its citizens, the tragedies that occur at the border precisely because of the broken system that has been in effect for decades, and, yes, the legitimate desire of the American people as expressed through the democratic process—a Catholic can say without any hesitation, "Something there is at this point in time that *does* love a wall," and vote accordingly. And if Mexico pays for it directly or indirectly, well, that ain't bad either. In a sense, they probably are doing so as we speak, but in a way that is collaborative, through their deployment of troops at their own northern and southern borders. They themselves are serving as the wall. Good fences do make good neighbors, and sometimes good neighbors make good fences.

One Mexican-American Catholic's Thoughts on Legal Versus Illegal Immigration

On some positions, cowardice asks the question, is it expedient? And then expedience comes along and asks the question, is it politic? Vanity asks the question, is it popular? Conscience asks the question, is it right? There comes a time when one must take the position that is neither safe nor politic nor popular, but he must do it because conscience tells him it is right.[13]

Martin Luther King, Jr.

What I am about to say is not safe, polite (or politic for that matter), or popular but what I believe is right as a practicing Catholic Christian.

There is a Catholic principle in moral theology which teaches that we can never do evil to bring about good. St. Paul clearly teaches this principle in Romans 3:8, and the *Catechism of the Catholic Church* also expresses this: "A good intention (for example, that of helping one's neighbor) does not make behavior that is intrinsically sinful and evil, such as lying and calumny, good or just. The end does not justify the means. Thus, the condemnation of an innocent person

---

[13]   Martin Luther King, "Remaining Awake Through a Great Revolution," Sermon delivered on Passion Sunday, March 31, 1968, in: *The Essential Writings and Speeches of Martin Luther King, Jr.*, p. 268, as cited in https://harpers.org/blog/2008/01/king-on-the-importance-of-conscience-in-action/.

cannot be justified as a legitimate means of saving the nation. On the other hand, an added bad intention (such as vainglory) makes an act evil that, in and of itself, can be good (such as almsgiving)."[14] Let me apply St. Paul's principle to the issue of illegal immigration. Most simply, you cannot do evil—*that is, break the immigration law and cross the border*—in order to bring about good—*to work and make money to send it back home.*

What is not mentioned is that a Latino man who leaves his country of origin will now leave his kids fatherless and his wife without the physical presence and protection of her husband. This Latino male will now enter the United States by himself, replete with every temptation under the sun to the tenth power. Let's be realistic, after an illegal immigrant in this country pays his rent, utilities, groceries, postage, vehicle, gas, et cetera, how much money does he actually send his family? Isn't it better to remain physically present with your family and grind it out together in your country of origin? *The family that prays together stays together.* Yes, families need money to survive, but what's more important is to have their father and husband physically present with them to teach them virtue, even in conditions of poverty. A man's vocation is to lead, protect, and provide for his family spiritually and physically.

What is more, imagine the temptations that arise. "It is not good that the man should be alone" (Gn 2:18). Bigamy is a huge problem in the Latino community amongst illegal immigrants; having a family in the United States and a

---

[14] CCC 1753.

family in South America is common. Just ask any Catholic priest who hears confessions and ministers in a Latino parish. It's the elephant in the living room that nobody wants to talk about.

The two main categories in this debate are legal immigrants and illegal immigrants. Those that believe in the rule of law and lawbreakers. The government has a moral and legal obligation to protect the due process rights of the people who immigrate here legally, and, on the flip side, they have the right to prevent the immigration of those who cross our borders illegally. This is not anti-immigration; in fact, it's very pro-immigration. It is not Catholic or Christian to advocate for irresponsible immigration. Immigration, to truly be a win-win for immigrants and the host country, requires order, knowledge, and balance.

There are many honest people from different countries (Mexico included) that are trying to follow the rules and immigrate to this country legally, but their application is kept from ever being processed because our country is being overrun by illegal immigrants mainly from the southwest. Our schools, jails, welfare rolls, hospitals, and labor market are being pushed to the limit, in large part because of this influx of illegal immigrants. The cost of providing social, medical, law enforcement and educational services to illegal aliens from every level of government is estimated at an astounding $135 billion per year.[15]

---

15   Paul Bedard, "Record $135 billion a year for illegal immigration, average $8,075 each, $25,000 in NY," *Washington Examiner*, September 27, 2017, https://www.washingtonexaminer.com/record -135-billion-a-year-for-illegal-immigration-average-8-075-each -25-000-in-ny.

I know that some people get offended when they hear the word "alien." However, the word "alien" is used in the Holy Bible as a descriptive word for a "stranger" or someone from another family or clan. The Mexican Constitution also uses the word "alien" for non-Mexican citizens.

I am Mexican-American; my parents are from Mexico, and the majority of my family is from Mexico or lives in Mexico. I am a retired LA Deputy Sheriff; my wife is a retired LA County nurse, and we have seen this abuse first-hand. Many Mexicans have a difficult time accepting this truth simply because we see this in terms of skin color and race instead of objectively. Our race becomes the apex of victimhood, and our brown skin becomes our truth, even above our Christianity. Most Latinos believe that those who oppose illegal immigration do so out of racism because this is the constant narrative they hear from the Hispanic and English mainstream media, both of which are studied practitioners of fake news delivery.

The Democratic Party benefits from illegal immigration because they pander to them by promising entitlements, thereby gaining their support. That is why Spanish radio talk show host Eddie Sotelo was able to marshal one million Hispanics to protest in the streets of Los Angeles over an immigration bill in California in 2006. I have no doubt that many of the protesters were illegal. But is the United States not entitled to control its immigration policy?

Consider Mexico, our southern neighbor whose leaders often lecture us about immigrant rights. Mexico's Constitution strictly forbids non-citizens from protesting against the Mexican government. "Foreigners may not in any way participate in the political affairs of the country" (Article 33). "Only citizens of the Republic may take part in the political affairs of the country" (Article 9).[16]

The Mexican constitution expressly forbids non-citizens from participating in the country's political life. Non-citizens are forbidden to participate in demonstrations or express opinions in public about domestic politics. In other words, no such mass demonstration would have been allowed in the streets of Mexico City.

What about religious values? Can I reconcile my convictions about illegal immigration as a Catholic? The *Catechism of the Catholic Church* does not support *illegal immigration*; the Church does support immigration reform, as does President Trump. The Church is encouraging and praying that a just resolution is found and enacted, as should we all. We should always pray for and enact the corporal works of mercy towards our fellow human beings; this is the golden rule given by Our Lord Jesus Christ.

But the fact is that the *Catechism* says that all immigrants are called to obey the laws of the country that has taken them in. Unfortunately, many of the baptized are uninformed Catholics who don't read the *Catechism* or the Bible. Therefore, they get caught up in leftist political causes because they listen to the left-wing propaganda from the Spanish-language media and are led by the nose by their neighbors and that media, a classic case of the blind leading the blind as Our Lord Jesus stated (cf. Mt 15:14).

---

[16]   "Political Constitution of the United Mexican States," http://comp arativeconstitutionsproject.org/wp-content/uploads/UNAM -Mexican-Constitution_vf.pdf?6c8912.

The vast majority of Mexican-Americans (like myself) have no problem with immigration; we are a country of immigrants, but many of us, and our numbers are growing every day, do have a problem with illegal immigration. I don't want illegal Arabs, Nigerians, Russians, Armenians, Chinese, Vietnamese, Brazilians, Irish, Syrians, Iraqis, or Mexicans. It is wrong to enable people to have contempt for laws. We are a country that functions much more efficiently than any other country because of the *rule of law*. Lax immigration laws encourage a lawless society.

Catholics should be against anything that is illegal in a free society (provided the law is just)! I find no contradiction between my Catholic faith and my support for the rule of law. Of course, we have to protect the dignity of every human person, which I believe US immigration law does. Every country has the right to define its own borders and to develop laws to defend them.

In closing, I'd like to relay a little-known and even less reported fact. Caesar Chavez, that great labor leader of the Mexican-American and Mexican national farmworkers, was a longtime foe of illegal immigration.

> Chavez himself was a third generation American citizen and a Navy veteran. Although he has become over time virtually the patron saint of the *Reconquista* movement to reclaim all of the southwest for Mexico, in his prime he was an ardent opponent of illegal immigration and actively fought against the importation of strikebreakers from Mexico. . . .

In 1979 testimony to Congress, Chavez complained, ". . . when the farm workers strike and their
strike is successful, the employers go to Mexico and
have unlimited, unrestricted use of illegal alien strikebreakers to break the strike. And, for over 30 years, the
Immigration and Naturalization Service has looked the
other way and assisted in the strikebreaking. I do not
remember one single instance in 30 years where the
Immigration service has removed strikebreakers. . . .
The employers use professional smugglers to recruit
and transport human contraband across the Mexican
border for the specific act of strikebreaking."[17]

The article further notes how, in 1969, Chavez led a march
to the border to protest illegal immigration. He "demanded
that the federal government close the border, routinely
reported suspected illegal immigrants to immigration officials, and put his brother in charge of Minutemen like border patrols which on more than one occasion resulted in the
beatings of intruders."

Some people will undoubtedly ask me: "Jesse, how can
you as a Mexican-American speak out like this and expose
all of Mexico's unjust immigration laws? You need to back
up the race!"

I don't look at the world through race bifocals. I look at
life with the heart of a Catholic Christian. We are saved by
grace not by race. To paraphrase Nazi concentration camp

---

prisoner and survivor Victor Frankl, from his book *Man's Search for Meaning*, "There are only two races of men, decent men and indecent men." We should never lower the bar for anyone; we should always set the bar high and encourage each other to take the moral high ground.

JR

Broader Questions of War and Peace

Donald John Trump was elected, in part, because he made clear his opposition to the wars and misadventures in which the country has found itself for the past couple of decades. He has called them "stupid" on more than one occasion and has expressed his desire to bring the troops home.

But he is no dove, as recent events have made crystal clear. Rather, he is a true America First candidate, and in his stated judgment, those wars did nothing to benefit the United States or its citizens, especially those who lost lives, limbs, or loved ones.

As is usually the case, his instincts were correct, as has been revealed through the so-called Afghanistan Papers. The waste and mismanagement involved and the outright falsehoods told by the powers that be (yes, including some top military brass for those inclined to an uncritical worship of anything that emanates from a general's mouth or pen) related to that conflict are in one sense stunning, and in another not surprising.

There has been no shortage of criticism from both the non-establishment Left and Right with regards to much that has transpired in our country since the 9/11 attacks. Unfortunately, the respective politicians and/or media outlets that voiced such concerns are not normally a significant part of that Washington establishment or the mainstream media and, hence, have a fraction of the platform that the uniparty pro-war voices have enjoyed. There, in the Swamp, with regards to foreign policy, there had often been unanimity in favor of more war until Donald Trump came along.

We Catholics have a rich tradition of just war teaching to draw upon when evaluating the legitimacy of any military efforts. This is not the place to go into a detailed analysis of just war theory and apply each article to events of the past twenty years. Rather, we shall present them and let the reader consider before making some further observations. The following passage from the *Catechism* highlights the conditions necessary for a war to be considered just.

> The fifth commandment forbids the intentional destruction of human life. Because of the evils and injustices that accompany all war, the Church insistently urges everyone to prayer and to action so that the divine Goodness may free us from the ancient bondage of war.
>
> All citizens and all governments are obliged to work for the avoidance of war. . . .
>
> The strict conditions for *legitimate defense by military force* require rigorous consideration. The gravity of such a decision makes it subject to rigorous conditions of moral legitimacy. At one and the same time:

—the damage inflicted by the aggressor on the nation or community of nations must be lasting, grave, and certain;

—all other means of putting an end to it must have been shown to be impractical or ineffective;

—there must be serious prospects of success;

—the use of arms must not produce evils and disorders graver than the evil to be eliminated. The power of modern means of destruction weighs very heavily in evaluating this condition.

These are the traditional elements enumerated in what is called the "just war" doctrine.[18]

Paragraphs 2307 and 2308 indicate a clear preference for peace that should characterize all Catholics, and truly all men of good will. War is to be avoided at all costs, or nearly all costs.

That said, consider our country's record militarily with regards to the last two of the criteria listed above: *there must be serious prospects of success; the use of arms must not produce evils and disorders graver than the evil to be eliminated.*

There must be serious prospects of success? The Afghanistan Papers reveal what many critics of the wars suspected all along: our leaders, both civilian and military, did not have a clear concept of what "success" would even look like. Forgive us for being so blunt, but a large swath of the "Right" in the country swoon and leave all critical judgment aside when a man in uniform tells them something.

There is a certain jingoism that pervades the Right in

---

18   CCC 2307–9.

this country, especially when it comes to matters of war and peace. ("Colloquially, jingoism is excessive bias in judging one's own country as superior to others—an extreme type of nationalism."[19] We would add that the sincere patriotism of the people is often cynically manipulated by the powers that be, through jingoism, to rush us into war. We don't count President Trump's extreme type of nationalist rhetoric as jingoistic because he has pledged to strive to keep us out of foolish wars. Tough talk and a clear willingness to back it up seems to have worked thus far. Remember the phrase "This ends now.")

As opposed to true patriotism, jingoism is unreflective, uncritical, and ultimately, dangerous, often to the very people who have followed our nation's leaders in beating the drums for war. Sadly, it is precisely those followers whose children for the most part have gone to die and be maimed overseas; the sons and daughters of the political class, with a few noteworthy exceptions, rarely pay that price. Think back to the great song by Creedence Clearwater Revival, "Fortunate One."

To question some of our foreign policy decisions and disasters is in no way to denigrate the troops. Rather, to question, forthrightly and honestly, the decisions that send young people off to die in a foreign country or to call for their return home when warranted is, in fact, to support them in the best possible way.

It is worth considering what our foreign policy, led by the Republican neocons and the Clinton wing of the

---

Democratic Party—in other words, "the Swamp" or "the uniparty"—has wrought in the Middle East and beyond on a country by country basis. Their disastrous record on foreign policy, these two Catholics believe, is reason enough to never let them approach the levers of power again, for they have played on the patriotism of so many Americans to deleterious effect.

Iraq

After 9/11, we were told by the Bush administration and others that Saddam Hussein had weapons of mass destruction and that somehow a Sunni Ba'athist strongman who was a mortal enemy of radical Islamic jihadists and the Iranian regime was the one behind the Twin Towers atrocity. He was not; we were lied into war by the establishment, a war that resulted in death and destruction for Christians and Yazidis. Yes, we did that. We, the United States of America. We may not have waged war on them, but we created the conditions under which they could be terrorized.

The country was thrown into turmoil. Its Christian and Yazidi population, protected from Islamic extremism by Hussein (We should not have to say this, but to acknowledge that fact should not earn one the accusation of being a fan of Saddam Hussein.), was decimated, and the country fell into the sphere of Iran, which was no surprise given the Shia majority. It is difficult to fathom how our political and military leaders could not have predicted as much. Pat Buchanan saw it coming, as did many other war skeptics on the Left and the Right. On the other hand, perhaps it is not so hard to fathom given what has been and remains to be learned from the Afghanistan Papers. Is it any wonder that skepticism of our military adventures played a significant role in Trump's victory in 2016?

And yet, while the finishing touches were being put on this book, Trump was faced with a situation that presented a unique problem for a president that had been elected on an anti-war platform, or at least an anti-stupid-war platform. Every person reading this undoubtedly knows the particulars, at least as reported, of the drone strike that killed Quassem Soleimani and the, to date, rather tepid response by the Iranians.

Those who elected Trump largely because of his promises not to lead us into any foolish wars were very concerned. Democrats and Never Trump Republicans leaped at the chance to say he was starting World War III, while others celebrated—perhaps reflexively, perhaps not—this show of American strength; such people seem to never hear of a missile attack or bombing that they dislike. And Trump, with his bellicose rhetoric over the years, certainly can feed into that atmosphere.

And yet, what happened? The Iranian response to Soleimani's killing was tepid at best, or worst as the case may be. Tragically, they shot down a passenger plane leaving their country and immediately lost whatever good will they may have had in terms of "victim status" among the international community. One wonders if the truth of that downing will ever come out.

But again, what happened? Full disclosure: the authors are always confused when we are told that the Shia Iranians are the number one state sponsor of terrorism around the globe when all the most prominent terror attacks, beheadings, genocides, and the like in the last few years have been committed by Sunni Muslims: ISIS, Boko Haram, Al Queda, the list goes on and on. And Iranian and other Shia forces, along with Russia (that arch-villain), have played a very prominent role in rolling back ISIS in countries like Syria. And yet, as individuals who voted for Trump partly because of his anti-stupid war stance, we trust him, and we hope for the best. Why? How can we say that?

Soleimani had been the head of the Quds force. Quds is the Arabic word for Jerusalem; does that mean that they won't rest until they have taken Jerusalem? Certainly, their calls for death to Israel and death to the United States qualify as longstanding indicators of hostile intent. Maybe instead of worrying about being thrown into a great war, we should realize that they have been at war with us since the Iranian Revolution of 1979. If Donald Trump decides to engage this war by targeting terrorist leaders instead of sending young Americans to die in foreign lands, if he is not only against stupid wars but against fighting wars stupidly and can achieve a lasting peace through strength, if by doing so, the tragic history of the middle eastern script can be rewritten for future generations, well, perhaps there is something to be said for his approach. That said, we implore President Trump to always make the case to the public for any military actions as clearly and convincingly as possible, to say nothing of Congress. Do not rest on the assertions of the "hawks" in your administration. We voted for you, in part, because of your resistance to the neocon warmongers. Honor your base by trusting us to really explain things and make the case.

Syria

Bashar Al-Assad, an Alawite, is another example of a Middle Eastern strongman who provided relative peace and prosperity for his people, Muslim and Christian, and kept Islamic extremism at bay until, that is, US backed "rebels" rose against him. Western propaganda notwithstanding, there is ample evidence that those "freedom fighters" that we supported, and with whom some anti-Trump politicians visited and were photographed before he took office, were jihadis. If you read the *Benghazi Brief*, you know what we are talking about. Again, the United States, in working to undermine a secular regime in the Middle East, paved the way for the horrors imposed by ISIS on our Christian brothers and sisters. Our record under the administrations before that of Donald Trump was remarkably consistent: Muslim spring always and everywhere equals Christian winter.

And yet, before Donald Trump, uniparty conservative and liberal alike supported those policies and the destruction of the Assad regime. Many in his administration still do, and yet, what actually happened on the ground was that everywhere the Assad regime lost control, ISIS terrorized the native Christian population, killing men, raping and enslaving women and children. Conversely, whenever and wherever Assad's armed forces and their allies retook territory, Mass would be celebrated again, Christmas trees went up, and the people sang songs. Is our media telling us the truth?

Are our military and political leaders? What do local Christians think? The following brief interview with Patriarch Ignatius Joseph III Younan took place in 2016.

Interviewer: What was life like for Christians under Assad?

Patriarch: We have to say clearly and honestly that chaos in whatever country of the Middle East, doesn't help in any way minorities, especially Christians, who are the most vulnerable segment of the population. In fact, Christians lack numbers and the oil and have no terroristic intent to pose any danger to civilized societies. They have been easily singled out by those bands of terrorists in the name of Islam. Therefore, a strong regime of government, like the one Syria had, (i.e., Assad's government) is far better than the one spreading death and destruction for over five years! The Western agglomerate media did succeed to demonize Assad, only because of the opportunistic greed of some politicians. . . . In both countries, Syria and Iraq, there will be no hope for a Christian survival, without a strong civilized state.

I: How do Christians in the Middle East view the United States and its actions?

P: We have to distinguish between politicians running the country and the American people. The latter are compassionate and ready to help the poor and the marginalized. Christians as well as most of the Middle Eastern population consider the United States Politics one of the worst. [Again, this interview was conducted in 2016, so before the Trump administration. Here, the patriarch criticizes the prior administrations.] You cannot help people by attempting to export and impose a kind of western democracy. This is a fiction, in countries where no separation of State and Religion is taken into consideration.

I: How do you view the Western Media?

P: Since the beginning of the turmoil in the region, Western Media have been very biased. History will judge . . . the lies of the western media conglomerate.

I: How do Christians of the Middle East view Russia, especially that country's actions compared to those of the US? Which country do they consider to be the greater friend and/or protector?

P: Christians and many other honest people consider Russia more reliable and sincere in defending the Syrian people in their national country. In this sense, Russia is more friendly and much more to be trusted! Despite its geo-political interests, Russia has often declared their intention and sought to help reach a political solution and preserve the unity of the country. If we want to talk about protection, Christians feel they have been abandoned, even betrayed by the Western politicians, not by the Russians.

I: What can concerned Christians in the United States and the West do to help your people?

P: To be truthful, to proclaim "Truth in Charity" as Pope Benedict XVI used to remind us. We urge Christians in the United States to wake up and defend the right of each people to find the appropriate way to govern themselves.

We pray and beg the "Theotokos", the Most Blessed Virgin Mary, who is invoked by our syriac hymns as "The Mother Full of Mercies", to look at us, her children, who have been the witnesses of Her Divine Son to the point of shedding their blood as martyrs. That we may survive!

If you don't believe the Christian patriarchs of the Middle East who have to live among people who wish their destruction, search online for the terms "Assad and Christians" and click to images. Look at the pictures that come up on your computer. Don't believe your lying eyes, believe our lying political class and media pundits if you prefer. But you are no friend to the Christians of the Middle East if you do. Those images you will see include pictures of Syrian Christian boy scouts marching and holding pictures of Assad, as well as others of him and his beautiful wife visiting Christian churches. Contrast that with what happened to those people after we assisted the "rebels." Carnage.

Assad is retaking his nation's territory, and the country is in the process of being rebuilt. May the United States under a Trump administration not interfere with or impede that process. Mr. President, as this is being written, Turkey is massing troops and tanks near the city of Idlib. Please consider the pleas of the leaders of the Christians in the Middle East and do not take part in regime change there. Is Turkey truly an ally of ours? Is that our fight? Please listen to the Christian leaders and take their fears and concerns into account. (The latest developments have Erdogan, the president of Turkey, opening the floodgates to Europe again for retreating anti-Assad forces . . . no doubt many jihadists among them. With friends like that . . . !)

Lybia

Gaddafi: a Muslim, but not Islamist, strongman who the United States establishment in its infinite wisdom decided had to go. Granted, Gaddafi had been guilty of acts of terrorism in the past but had seemed to have found a modus vivendi with the West. Like the others, he was the mortal enemy of the radical Islamists. Why, one wonders, did the United States and others decide that he had to be eliminated? But no matter, eliminated he was, despite his warnings to the West along the lines of "After me the flood" (of Muslim refugees into Europe). Those warnings proved prescient, for Libya served as the cork that kept hundreds of thousands of Muslims, many radicals among them, from flowing into Europe. To paraphrase Joe Biden bragging about his forcing the Ukrainian prosecutor to drop an investigation into his son's company: "Well, son of a bitch," Gaddafi was right. The Islamic incursion into a post-Christian Europe is already bearing hideous fruit, and it will only get worse. It is difficult to look optimistically on the situation given demographic realities. Another feather in the cap of the foreign policy establishment that Donald Trump railed against!

A final thought on a proper Catholic course for our great country (and we write that in all sincerity) to take with regards to our "regime change" efforts in the Middle East and their consequences which should have been foreseen. Some readers may recognize this as the Act of Contrition, said most commonly after confessing one's sins. Under President Trump, it is hoped that we will make satisfaction for those sins.

> O, my God, I am heartily sorry for having offended thee, and I detest all my sins because of thy just punishments, but most of all because they offend thee, my God, who art all good and deserving of all my love. With the help of thy grace, I resolve to sin no more and to avoid the near occasion of sin.

Russia

Russia! Russia! Russia! (Apologies to Jan Brady.) Donald Trump was elected president without any help from Russia, notwithstanding the claims of Democrats, Never Trump Republicans, and most of the media. Amazingly, they continue to make that discredited assertion today (at the time of writing) at the president's impeachment trial. Mueller's special counsel proved there was no collusion, and they were not friendly witnesses or investigators. The trials that are coming (perhaps already here by the time you read this) related to that biggest scandal in American political history will, it is hoped, prove what happened. But beyond the travesty and criminality of the particulars involved, for our purposes here, we would like to observe a few things about Russia that go largely unreported in the Western media, even by those in favor of Trump because, well, Russia is, of course, enemy number one and must remain as such.

First, Catholics may be interested to know that Christianity is growing remarkably in Russia. The Russian Orthodox Church has a close friend and supporter in Vladimir Putin. Putin, in fact, is on record as saying he will protect, nay, fight to protect Christians in areas throughout the world where they are threatened. He has backed up that pledge in places like Syria, where Russian forces have been instrumental in eradicating ISIS.

We Catholics must ask ourselves: why is peace with Russia not possible? Trump and Putin seemed to have a certain rapport. The corrupt political establishment, again both Right and Left, is for some reason terrified of any rapprochement between the two countries. Trump, in his informal common-sense way, asked many times on campaign, would it be a bad thing to get along with Russia? Apparently, for too many in the foreign policy establishment, and, truth be told, it seems in Trump's administration as well, the answer is yes. And so, Russia is and has been demonized.

But our opinion is that, in the wake of the fall of the Soviet Union, Russia has been more sinned against than sinning vis-à-vis the West. Please don't stop reading. Remember Belloc's admonition to read widely, even, perhaps especially, views with which you may not agree.

Every thinking person should read the work on Russia by Stephen F. Cohen. A contributing editor for *The Nation* magazine, a journal of the hard Left undoubtedly, Cohen provides a view on Russia that should be read and considered by all Americans. He is also a frequent guest of Tucker Carlson on television.

Professor Cohen has written in great detail of the suffering the Russian people endured in the wake of the fall of Communism, suffering brought about in large measure by Western advisors and a new breed of Russian oligarchs—in other words, by our old friends "the global elite." Cohen's writing over the years serves as an eye-opener and goes a long way towards explaining the popularity of Vladimir Putin. Suffice to say, the West, specifically the "global elite" of the West, bears much of the responsibility for the corruption under Yeltsin and the rise of the oligarchs. Vladimir Putin is the Russian people's answer to that crisis.

In international relations, the West has pressured Russia in ways in which it promised not to; after the end of the Cold War, the West pledged not to advance NATO towards Russia's doorstep, and it has gone back on its word and done exactly that. Russia is always painted as the bad guy, but in our view, the West has much to answer for, probably more even than Putin and company. And we are not alone; other Catholics, such as Pat Buchanan, feel similarly. Consider the words of Daniel J. Mahoney, a professor at Assumption College in Worcester, Massachusetts. "We also need to examine our role in the deterioration of East-West relations. We know the Russians have made many mistakes and are perhaps unduly suspicious of Western intentions. That said, the United States massively intervened in the 1996 Russian presidential elections to support Boris Yeltsin, who was presiding over a kleptocracy that betrayed the promise of post-communist reform and was shamelessly impoverishing tens of millions of ordinary Russian citizens."[20]

It is to be hoped that Donald Trump, no Russian agent he, but rather a man who seeks peace and prosperity and does not subscribe to the neocon pieties that have ravaged the world, will find a way to "make a deal" and, thus, a lasting peace with Russia.

Ukraine

The United States under the Obama administration had a pernicious influence on Ukraine, and our actions resulted in a civil war, which led to the incursion by Russia and the consequent annexation of Crimea (voted upon by the Crimeans themselves mind you, overwhelmingly so). So, forgive us if we hold the applause for our patriotic members of the Department of State, those "dedicated public servants" trotted out during the House portion of the impeachment spectacle.

Again, this book is a Catholic look at Trump, take it as you will, and these few paragraphs are contrarian looks at our foreign policy in Ukraine, again, take them as you will. But here it is, what we think happened. The United States fomented a coup there because the government under a man named Yanukovych was tilting more towards Russia rather than NATO; perhaps Russia was offering them a better deal,

---

[20]   Daniel J. Mahoney, "Post-Communist Russia Is Not the Soviet Union," *RealClear Politics*, August 7, 2018, https://www.realclear politics.com/articles/2018/08/07/post-communist_russia_is_ not_the_soviet_union_137730.html.

but the United States played a key role in fomenting the so-called Maidan Revolution that ousted Yanukovych and installed someone friendly to our misguided and illegal project. The aforementioned Mahoney, in the same article, supports this view of those events. He writes, "Few realize that however unsavory, the democratically elected government of Ukraine that was overthrown in February 2014 should not have been assaulted by mobs with the express support of the U.S. government. That makes a mockery of democracy promotion."

The most positive thing that can be said of this entire sad escapade is that this wonderful exportation of something akin to "our democracy" led, finally and happily, to the election of reformer Zelensky. But know that the State Department holdovers from the Obama regime were none too pleased with that outcome. Nor was Joe Biden. This story, however, is better told in the narrative on the impeachment sham since Ukraine was at the center of that travesty.

Iran

For Trump supporters who were enthusiastic about his stated opposition to foreign entanglements and misadventures, recent events in Iraq involving Iran were concerning, no doubt. Trump and his team however have satisfactorily made the case, at least to us, that this has been a slow-burning war with Iran since the Islamic Republic came into being at the end of the Carter administration, a silent war, perhaps, in which we have simply ceded ground as Iran and its proxies have made gains around the globe. The rhetoric of the Iranian regime has always been death to Israel and death to the United States. Well, Trump decided enough was enough and that "this ends now." Averse to losing even a single American life over there, he has also decided that the best way to end this saga is by the targeted killing of the terrorist leaders of our enemies. Baghdadi, head of ISIS and mourned by the anti-Trump press as an "austere religious scholar," and then Soleimani, head of the Iranian Quds Force and the key supporter of Hezbollah throughout the globe.

One wonders what the next few years will hold in the arena of US-Iran relations. Of course, they are inextricably tied to what happens with Israel. But we trust Trump more than we trusted Obama, more than we would have trusted Hillary, and more than anyone who will oppose him in 2020. With the killing of Soleimani, Trump told the Iranians, "This ends now."

China

Trump has for years been telling anyone and everyone that China is "killing us on trade." And he called out those responsible. As his first term comes to a close, he has achieved a great victory for our country: a new trade deal with China that will go a long way towards rebalancing the books and flowing investment into the United States. That translates into jobs, good ones too. Trump used the leverage of the United States markets and his favorite cudgel, tariffs, but also his considerable charm and relationship with President Xi to good effect. He appoints good men on foreign trade—no, great men in their sphere—in Wilbur Ross, Bob

Lighthizer, and Peter Navarro to represent the United States and our interests, and has a prominent Catholic point man in Larry Kudlow to explain it to the American people.

North Korea

North Korea seems to have faded a bit from the spotlight, but the steps taken by President Trump and Kim Jong Un in the DMZ were hugely significant. Time will tell, but our president, with his seemingly inexhaustible supply of energy, thinks outside the box and accomplishes great things, that others would not even consider. Which observation leads into . . .

Israel

Israel and its place in the Middle East and the world has been the locus of near-constant political unrest and violence since its establishment. The problem could very well be said to be intractable. How could it be otherwise when some of its neighbors openly declare their intent to one day, soon and very soon they hope, wipe Israel from the face of the earth. One can acknowledge injustices against Palestinians as well. But, for our purposes here, we need not wade into that discussion.

To some extent, without minimizing the vast human suffering that has occurred on both sides, it matters not how we got to this point. Here we are. What are we going to do about it? What are they going to do about it? Donald Trump is without a doubt a great friend of Israel and is not impartial in this matter.

But if he cannot be impartial, does that preclude him from being fair-minded? He is a problem solver; he wants to solve this decades-old problem that seems insoluble. And so to that end, as his impeachment trial was drawing to a close in the Senate, he unveiled a proposed plan that included a two-state solution, always thought to be a non-starter for Israel. And yet, there was Bibi Netanyahu standing with him as it was introduced to the media and the world.

In keeping with our effort to draw on sources not overly friendly toward President Trump, consider the observations recorded by Scott Ritter in an op-ed published online at *RT*.[21]

The specifics of the proposed deal can be easily found online. What Ritter gets at, however—remember this is no particular friend of Donald Trump or Israel—is that this is a "this ends now" type of deal. The insane position of the state of Israel vis-à-vis its neighbors and the tragic situation of the Palestinians has bedeviled the world for decades. Through this deal, Trump endeavors to get the Islamic world to abjure Islamic terror and threats directed against Israel. Ritter writes of the various security guarantees "and related preconditions that a Palestinian government must agree to, including the disarmament of Hamas and other militant groups."

Ritter acknowledges that the deal just might work because

---

21   Scott Ritter, "Trump's 'Deal of the Century' is an 'offer they can't refuse', and that's why it will likely work," *RT*, January 28, 2020, https://www.rt.com/op-ed/479422-israel-palestine-deal-ultima tum/.

Trump has set the clock a-ticking. The ball is in the court of the Palestinians and their allies; if, after four years, no deal is agreed to, implicit in the offer is the expectation that Israel will settle the issue, under surely worse terms than those currently on offer.

Ritter seems to applaud Trump for imposing his vision for peace in the Middle East upon both parties. Previously, Palestinian statehood was an unconditional demand of the Palestinians, a demand historically and consistently rejected out of hand by Israel. In providing for that statehood, Donald Trump "has done what no other has been able to accomplish — get Israel to agree to a two-state solution with Palestine. With the fail-safe ultimatum he's concocted, the Palestinians may yet end up getting on board."

Donald Trump is an America First president, no doubt. But given the United States' role in the world, we unavoidably have many engagements, friendly and not so friendly, that fall under the banner of foreign policy. We are two Catholics who think that, in general, our foreign policy establishment should have to "make the case" much more often and more persuasively than they do. The genie is out of the bottle. We understand the need for certain things remaining classified, but too many claims are made but left as naked assertions, and actions taken which please half the country and enrage the other half, always along partisan lines. If our government vis-à-vis foreign policy is more transparent with us, it is to be hoped that that will less frequently be the case. Consider this an appeal to President Trump to continue to seek peace through strength and diplomacy in the world.

7

I WILL ROUT
YOU OUT

*It's not that we don't have enough scoundrels to curse; it's
that we don't have enough good men to curse them.*

G. K. Chesterton[1]

THE impassioned words spoken so frequently by President Trump and his entire style of campaigning featuring
plain-speaking and rough talk reminds one of another tough
figure from America's political past, "Old Hickory" Andrew
Jackson. Read these words attributed to Jackson and see if
you hear echoes of a Trump speech about the Swamp:

> Gentlemen! I too have been a close observer of the
> doings of the Bank of the United States. I have had
> men watching you for a long time, and am convinced
> that you have used the funds of the bank to speculate
> in the breadstuffs of the country. When you won, you
> divided the profits amongst you, and when you lost,
> you charged it to the bank. You tell me that if I take
> the deposits from the bank and annul its charter I shall

---

[1] "Quotations of G. K. Chesterton," *The Apostolate of Common
Sense*, https://www.chesterton.org/quotations-of-g-k-chesterton/.

ruin ten thousand families. That may be true, gentle-
men, but that is your sin! Should I let you go on, you
will ruin fifty thousand families, and that would be my
sin! **You are a den of vipers and thieves. I have determined to rout you out, and by the Eternal,** (bringing
his fist down on the table) **I will rout you out!**

Strong words from Old Hickory, the seventh president of
the United States and a man no stranger to battle—in wars,
duels, and politics. Compare those with these from a speech
Donald Trump made in 2016 in Colorado:

Real change also means getting rid of the corruption
in Washington. . . .

. . . Public corruption is a grave and profound
threat to a democracy.

Government corruption spreads outward, like a
cancer, and infects the operations of government itself.
If the corruption is not removed, then the people are
not able to have faith in their government. It deadens
and saps the spirit of civic participation.

Corruption decays our trust in institutions and our
legal system.

When the outcome is fixed, when the system is
rigged, people lose hope. They detach. Our society
becomes unplugged and unhinged. When the powerful can get away with anything, because they have the
money and the connections to rig the system, then the
laws lose their moral authority. . . .

As FDR once said, government by organized money
is just as dangerous as government by organized mob.

This is what we often see in Third World countries — where the governments are often run by a small handful of corrupt people for their personal enrichment.

Corruption is corrosive to every institution of government, and it must be stopped.

Restoring honesty to our government, and the rule of law to our society, will be my highest priority as President. . . . That is why my Contract With The American Voter begins with a plan to end government corruption and take our country back from the special interests.

I want the entire corrupt Washington establishment to hear and to heed the words I am about to say. When we win on November 8th, We Are Going To Washington, D.C. **And We Are Going To DRAIN THE SWAMP!**[2]

This was as clear a declaration of war on the corrupt establishment as one could imagine. The establishment had already declared war on him. As these words are written, the impeachment trial in the United States Senate is in full swing. It is the culminating and, hopefully, last ditch effort of those who recognize in Donald Trump their mortal enemy, because in him they see a man determined to restore honesty and integrity to our government (which restoration would result in a raft of indictments, trials, and convictions

2   Sundance, "Transcript of Donald Trump in Colorado: 'Draining The Swamp,'" *The Last Refuge* (blog), October 29, 2016, https://theconservativetreehouse.com/2016/10/29/transcript-of-donald-trump-in-colorado-draining-the-swamp/.

of many in the Swamp), or just because they disagree with his view of what our foreign and domestic policies should be. With regards to foreign policy and the inane endless wars in the Middle East with no resolution, Trump appears to have said, "This ends now!" Similarly, with regards to being taken advantage of in foreign trade deals, he has said, "This ends now." And with regards to corruption in the United States government, he has likewise said, "This ends now." And so, like a cornered beast, the establishment set about to destroy him.

8

THE SWAMP
STRIKES BACK

Once the torch of treason is ignited everywhere, it ruins public order, fosters contempt of government, and stimulates lawlessness. It overthrows every element of sacred and civil power.[1]

Pope Gregory XVI

Treason?

Donald Trump, Tweet Sept. 5, 2018

I will not lie to you. These false attacks are absolutely hurtful. To be lied about, to be slandered, to be smeared so publicly, and before your family that you love, is very painful. What is going on is egregious beyond any words. People that know the story, people that see the story, people that know the facts, they can't even believe it. It's reprehensible beyond description, it's totally corrupt.[2]

---

[1]   Pope Gregory XVI, Encyclical *Singulari Nos* (1834), no. 4.
[2]   "TRANSCRIPT: Donald Trump's Speech Responding To Assault Accusations," NPR, October 13, 2016, https://www.npr.org/2016/10/13/497857068/transcript-donald-trumps-speech-responding-to-assault-accusations.

WHEN he made this speech, Trump, perhaps, may have had no idea of what was in store for him as president of the United States, or maybe he did. Our country has prided itself, in comparison with so many others around the world, on a long tradition of the peaceful transition of power. But the transition from Barack Obama to Donald Trump would see a dramatic break with that tradition. That which many in the mainstream media dismissed as crank conspiracy theory is now being revealed to have been true all along.

True it is that many bloggers, independent and part-time journalists, were onto the deep state and their machinations very early, the aforementioned Sundance among them. True it is also that a select few in the mainstream media such as Tucker Carlson, Sean Hannity, and Laura Ingraham and their guests John Solomon and Sara Carter also had the story, along with a network of "digital warriors" online.

True it is also, though, that it has been worse than we expected all along. What has been attempted is a coup by other means: the attempted take down of the winner of an election on spurious grounds, in violation of our laws.

The comportment of the most rabid anti-Trumpers, from the time of the lead up to the election through the impeachment charade and beyond, has been reprehensible and un-American. It is amazing and instructive to look back to the closing days of the 2016 campaign and see that a great concern of many on the Left was whether Donald Trump would accept the results of the election. They, themselves, have not accepted the results of that election. Again, they accuse him of precisely those things of which they themselves are guilty. We think that is called projection.

Resist, We Must

Granted, the anti-Trump side's refusal to accept his presidency is not all bad in that it has resulted in many moments of high humor for fans of the president. The famous video of the woman on her knees on inauguration day shrieking "Noooooooo!" at the sky is hilarious. The clips cobbled together online of the mainstream media talking heads on the night of the election are priceless. If you have not watched them, try to find one. Again, great stuff, and very revealing of the true bias of the "fake news." But sadly, there has been much that has occurred that is not funny at all.

The media has always emphasized the threat of violence from pro-Trump people. The exact opposite, however, is what has actually occurred. The vast (and we do mean vast) majority of politically motivated violence in the lead up to and in the wake of Trump's victory has been committed by anti-Trump individuals or groups. Consider just a few well-known incidents from 2016:

> **April 29** – Around 1,000 to 3,000 protested in the area surrounding Burlingame, California, where Trump was to give a speech at the California GOP convention. Protesters rushed security gates at one point. Activists blocked a main intersection outside the event and vandalized a police car. Eventually, the police restored order in the area. For safety reasons, Trump himself was forced to climb over a wall and enter through a back entrance of the venue.
>
> **June 2** – Protests and riots occurred outside a Trump rally in San Jose, California. During a series

of protests, hundreds of anti-Trump protesters waving Mexican flags climbed on cars, and harassed supporters of Donald Trump. There were reports of violence including instances of bottles being thrown and assaults against Trump supporters. A police officer was assaulted. At least one American flag was burned by protesters. Video footage went viral of a female Trump supporter being pelted by eggs thrown by protesters. The violence and police inaction was decried at San Jose City Hall later that month.

August 19 – Protesters harassed, pushed, and spit on Trump supporters outside a fundraising event in Minneapolis.[3]

Protests are one thing, but the violence directed at citizens for their support of a particular candidate is unprecedented in recent American political history, especially in its extension to actual political figures. Senator Rand Paul was physically assaulted by an anti-Trump neighbor and hospitalized with serious injuries; he feels the effects to this day. Paul was also at the congressional baseball game in 2017 when an anti-Trump man opened fire on the Republican team, wounding a number of individuals, most famously and seriously Congressman Steve Scalise of Louisiana. According to the Wikipedia account of the incident (citing an article from the *Daily Beast*), the shooter had written, "'Trump is a Traitor. Trump Has Destroyed Our Democracy. It's Time

---

3   Wikipedia, s.v. "Timeline of protests against Donald Trump," last modified February 20, 2020, 05:09, https://en.wikipedia.org/wiki/Timeline_of_protests_against_Donald_Trump.

to Destroy Trump & Co.' above his repost of a Change.org petition demanding "the legal removal" of Trump and Vice President Mike Pence for 'treason.'"[4]

We have seen the rise of a group called Antifa, which stands for—apparently the irony is unintentional—Anti-Fascist or Anti-Fascism. This is a masked group that has assaulted people, vandalized public property, and seems to be given a wide berth in a certain liberal city in the Pacific Northwest.

The word "Resist" and the concept of "The Resistance" have entered the American political vernacular. Those terms don't exactly indicate the acceptance of the result of a presidential election. Nor does the fact that a website dedicated to impeaching President Trump went live on his inauguration day as reported by the news outlets such as the *Washington Post* and *Time* magazine. Nor is the fact that our television viewing and internet surfing has been interrupted for too long by the ubiquitous Tom Steyer ads calling for his impeachment. It is to be hoped that with his withdrawal from the Democratic Primary, we will see less and less of him.

Again, this is not normal. As Catholics, we value public order and, yes, of course, legitimate political demonstration and protest, but the above-described actions of those

4   Wikipedia, s.v. "2017 Congressional baseball shooting," last modified February 21, 2020, 17:29, https://en.wikipedia.org/wiki/2017_Congressional_baseball_shooting; *Kelly Weill, Katie Zavadski, and Emma Kerr,* "Congressional Shooter Loved Bernie Sanders, Hated 'Racist & Sexist' Republicans," *The Daily Beast,* June 14, 2017, http://www.thedailybeast.com/congressional-shooter -loved-bernie-sanders-hated-racist-and-sexist-republicans.

opposed to Donald Trump can only be condemned by any sane, let alone decent, person.

The unprecedented nature of the opposition to candidate and then President Trump is also reflected in the actions of anti-Trump politicians and bureaucrats, the "deep state," who were threatened by the candidacy, election, and presidency of a man outside their control. Among those for whom the main source of news has been MSNBC or CNN, we perfectly well expect that many will immediately dismiss even the use of that term as the paranoid rhetoric of a conspiracy theorist. That is fine. However, we also perfectly well expect that there are those among that demographic who are open to what is being revealed now and will be unfolding in the coming months, perhaps even as you read this book. It is becoming increasingly apparent that there was an active conspiracy carried out by the highest figures in the previous administration to undermine Trump's candidacy and then his presidency, a plot not merely to undermine it, but to end it through weaponizing the intelligence apparatus of the United States in the furtherance of a non-violent coup.

A Coup in 280 Characters or Less[5]

One of the most keen and insightful observers of the entire sordid affair is a man named Brian Cates, a columnist for

---

[5]   For an outstanding and succinct summary of the FISA abuse aspects of the plot to bring down President Trump, view the videos at Sundance's site. They are produced by the same John Spiropolous whose videos on the Clinton server scandal we provided links to earlier and can be viewed at https://theconservativetreehouse.com/2018/03/19/why-how-who-the-big-picture-in-video-summary/.

The Epoch Times (https://www.theepochtimes.com/) and the investigative journalism website UncoverDC.com, who tweets as @drawandstrike.

Around the turn of the new year 2020, he posted a series of tweets which serves as a solid summary of just what was done to Donald Trump for the unpardonable offense of threatening to govern in the interest of Main Street Americans and then winning an election based on that promise. Well, when we put it that way, it seems more understandable why they would stop at nothing—their very existence was threatened, and no trick was too base for these people. Much of the information here is not known by those who have not followed the story closely or have watched only CNN or MSNBC. It may seem like the stuff of tinfoil hats and conspiracy theories. That is fine; your scribes can live with that. We are confident that in the coming weeks and months, the events described will be more widely known. So, here it is, an account of criminality, yes, an attempted coup, at the highest levels of our government condensed for your convenience. (The below is the article version of Cates' twitter thread published at UncoverDC.com.)[6]

---

6   Brian Cates, "A Retrospective on The Past Four Years of Fake News Trump Hysteria," UncoverDC, December 31, 2019, https://un coverdc.com/2019/12/31/a-retrospective-on-the-past-four-years -of-fake-news-trump-hysteria/.

A Retrospective on The Past Four Years
of Fake News Trump Hysteria

Thanks to Robert Mueller's final report and the report from DOJ's Inspector General Horowitz on the FBI's FISA abuses, we have a far clearer picture of what really happened during the 2016 election and the first three years of the Trump presidency.

Because Democrats and the DNC Media Complex won't tell you the truth, here's what really happened the last four years.

The Spying Begins

The SpyGate plotters in the FBI start spying on Donald Trump and his team in 2015. They claim they started in late July of 2016, but that's a lie.

Their spying is cloaked as a counterintelligence investigation. The FBI lies to the FISA Court saying they have "probable cause," alleging they have solid, verified evidence that Carter Page is acting as an agent of a foreign power. They also "suspect" Lt. Gen. Michael Flynn, George Papadopoulos and Paul Manafort are doing the same.

To get FISA warrants to spy on Trump's campaign, the FBI uses a fake Trump/Russia dossier. That dossier came from a Clinton political operative, former MI6 spy Christopher Steele. The spying continues after Trump wins the election. They spy on his transition team, and they spy after Trump enters the White House.

The FBI continues to make use of Steele's fake Trump/

Russia allegations even after becoming aware that Steele was being paid by the Hillary Clinton campaign to come up with damaging opposition research targeting the Trump campaign.

The FBI renews Page's warrant three times. This means they are doing "legal" electronic spying on Trump and his close associates for 11 months, from Oct '16 to Sept '17.

Exculpatory Evidence

During this time, the FBI accumulates exculpatory evidence about Page, Flynn, Manafort and Papadopoulos, but the agency withholds that evidence from the FISA Court in each of the three warrant renewal applications.

Investigators from the DOJ's Inspector General's Office [OIG] catch Kevin Clinesmith (the FBI lawyer in charge of handling the FISA warrant renewals) tampering with a CIA email. Reason: The FBI had asked the CIA if Page's claims about being a CIA contact were true. The CIA had affirmed to the FBI that Page was indeed an operational contact for their agency.

In fact, from 2008-2013, Page was working closely with the CIA in helping bust up a Russian spy ring. That continued well through the time period of the FISA warrant. So, yes, Page had been communicating with the CIA about his Russian contacts all the way up thru 2016-17.

Unfortunately, this response to the FBI's query is not what the SpyGate plotters want to hear.

How can the FBI continue using Page's contacts with Russian government and intelligence officials as evidence he's a Russian agent if Page is working with the CIA, briefing them about these contacts? To fix this problem, Clinesmith decides to edit the CIA's response to the FBI's query. He alters the email to show the CIA saying Page was not a contact for their agency.

Also, in January of 2017, the FBI finally gets around to interviewing Steele's main source for the allegations against Carter Page in the dossier. The source *completely disavows* Steel's allegations, which the FBI had used when obtaining the warrant.

The source tells the FBI that Steele was LYING to them because he – the source – never told Steele many of the allegations that appear in the Page FISA warrant. The source says that, at *best*, SOME of what Steele conveyed were *gross exaggerations*. The source is horrified to see Steele positioning their conversations as "covert intelligence" from a highly placed informant inside the Russian government.

Again, this is NOT what the SpyGate plotters want to hear, so they also withhold the source's testimony from the FISA Court.

To recap, the FBI is not only hiding what the CIA said about Page, they're also hiding what Steele's "source" told them.

Comey fired; Mueller hired

In May of 2017, FBI Director Comey is fired, so he leaks one of his memos to the New York Times. Comey gets called to testify before Congress where he DEMANDS the appointment of a Special Counsel to investigate Russian interference in the 2016 election. He demands a special focus on the Trump campaign's ties to Russia.

Former FBI Director Robert Mueller is tapped to be the Special Counsel. He assembles a team of 13 Angry Democrats and begins his investigation.

Two investigations meld into one. We have many of the members of the FBI's Crossfire Hurricane counterintelligence team converging with Mueller's Special Counsel on a quest for their Holy Grail: any evidence they can find of Trump crimes and/or Russian collusion.

In late September 2017, the last FISA renewal runs out and the Mueller Special Counsel is left without its influence on the hunt for their Holy Grail.

Despite the FBI's 11 months of intensive, super-wide surveillance of Trump & his associates, the Crossfire Hurricane team has NOTHING to hand off to Mueller. The only crimes identified turn out to be some bank/tax fraud crimes by Manafort and former Trump lawyer Michael Cohen, and a raft of process perjury charges against Flynn, Papadopoulos and Roger Stone.

Special counsel expands its search

Now all hope rests on Mueller's Special Counsel team, and they are gifted by US Deputy Attorney General Rod Rosenstein with a new super-duper wide scope of authority for their intensive and exhaustive investigation.

With that gift, Mueller and his pack of crack bloodhounds search far and wide, high and low, carefully looking behind every rock, bush and tree for 2 1/2 years. And they find … nothing. They even use that super-duper wide scope provided by Rosenstein to go frantically digging through long-deceased Fred Trump's estate taxes. Nothing.

Throughout this 2 1/2 year period that Mueller and his team of 13 angry Democrats are doing all this furious and futile searching, the Fake News Media is being fed a TON of fake leaks, and they regale the public with ribald tales of all the evidence they claim Mueller is finding! Mueller's team is doing everything but investigating what brought them there in the first place; the allegations within the Steele dossier. Mueller states that wasn't in his "purview".

Anonymous leakers string gullible news reporters along for years about how Trump's close associates are "flipping" on Trump and singing like canaries to Mueller as they expose all the secret coordination between Trump and his master in Moscow, Vladimir Putin.

According to some of these Fake News outlets, Trump is supposedly in a depression inside the White House, stumbling around in a stupor in his bathrobe, chugging Diet Coke and morosely watching The Gorilla Channel in an attempt to cheer himself up as the walls start closing in on him.

Schiff and Nunes

One bug-eyed crazy member of Congress (a Democrat, naturally) gets himself plenty of TV face time by making extravagant claims about all the good, solid, "more than circumstantial evidence" he's seen proving Trump/Russia Election Collusion. . . .

This crazy bug-eyed Democrat is also in a locked battle for two years with Republican Rep. Devin Nunes. Both men produce dueling memos in February of 2018 about claims of FBI abuse of the FISA system. . . .

Nunes' memo is released first, detailing serious abuses and problems with the Carter Page FISA warrant, alleging the FBI is hiding key information from the Court. Schiff's response memo is a repudiation of the Nunes memo, claiming Nunes is deliberately lying and misleading the public for his own partisan political purposes.

Which memo is truthful is a matter that remains unresolved all through 2018 and nearly all of 2019.

Fakers exposed

Meanwhile, the Mueller Special Counsel drags on. Attorney General Jeff Sessions resigns in late 2018 and is temporarily replaced by Matthew Whitaker. In February of 2019, Whitaker suddenly announces Mueller is wrapping up his investigation. Many media outlets and political commentators refuse to believe him.

It turns out Whitaker is telling the truth. Mueller really is ending his investigation, and the only unfinished business ends up being the sentencing of Manafort surrogate Richard Gates, and yet another useless process perjury charge against …Roger Stone.

Democrats and the Fake News Media scramble to adjust to the new reality while avoiding any accountability whatsoever. After more than two years of selling fake news about Mueller having real Trump/Russia Election Collusion evidence, the charlatans and fakers get exposed when Mueller releases his final report.

The best Mueller's team could do was a vague obstruction argument based on a gymnastic, pretzel-like reading of an obstruction-of-justice statute. With a case so weak he is unwilling to make a charge himself, Mueller punts it upstairs to the new Attorney General, William Barr.

Barr and Deputy Attorney General Rod Rosenstein look at Mueller's final offering, they have a good laugh, [dismiss] it, and go out for beer and pizza.

And that's what happened. The 2 1/2 year-long exhaustive investigation by Mueller's 13 Angry Democrats killed the Trump/Russia Collusion Hoax.

In all their pre-July 2016 spying they found no Trump crimes.

In all their post-July 2016 spying before they got the Page FISA warrant they found no Trump crimes.

In all their FISA spying from Oct '16 to Sept '17 they found no Trump crimes.

See a pattern emerging?

Finally, despite 13 Angry Democrats on Mueller's team investigating from June 2017 all the way to February of 2019 – they found … no Trump crimes.

Amazing, isn't it?

Ponder this. From the moment Trump announced his presidential run in 2015 to the moment he won the Presidency, Trump was THE most-thoroughly vetted Presidential candidate in US History.

You know they tried.

They tried and they failed.

A crime must be invented

If all that spying and intercepting and transcribing and circulating and investigating of Trump and his close associates for more than FOUR YEARS had produced ANYTHING REAL, you would have SEEN it by now.

This is why, by late Spring/early Summer of 2019, the Democrats and DNC Media realized if they were EVER going to get Trump impeached or successfully damage his re-election efforts, they would need to INVENT crimes.

So put yourselves in the shoes of the Democratic leadership and the DNC Media Complex back in April/May of [2019]. After almost four years of relentless searching, you can't find any real Trump crimes, but then the WRONG GUY wins the Presidency in Ukraine and you learn that Trump and Rudy Giuliani are working with this new President to look into massive corruption in his country. Their focus is on billions of US taxpayer dollars sent to Ukraine as foreign aid that just up and disappeared.

What to do?

If you are part of the Democratic Party leadership or among the executives in the DNC Media Complex, you INVENT a crime involving a phone call. This invented crime will then be "exposed" by a criminal leaker, but to keep it sounding legit, you will call this person a whistle blower.

Ironically, former Vice President Joe Biden got caught on video openly boasting about forcing the former Ukrainian government into a quid quo pro by threatening to withhold a $1 billion loan guarantee that had already been agreed to.

In other words, the fake crime the Democrats used as a catalyst for impeaching Trump is exactly what Biden is shown bragging about in the viral video. That's how incredulously absurd this all is.

Democrats do not want ANYBODY investigating what Biden and others did in Ukraine from 2012 to 2019. President Trump was doing his job: trying to enforce the law and honor treaties in an effort to discover where our taxpayer-funded foreign aid really went, but Democrats are lying about that activity, saying it's a CRIME.

This is how we got where we are at today with this absurd impeachment theater. Schiff continues telling bald faced lies, first denying his staff coordinated with the fake whistleblower, then admitting it but insisting he doesn't know the leaker's name.

And, after 2 months of babbling about extortion and bribery, Pelosi and company rolled out two absurd articles about "abuse of power" and "contempt of Congress."

It looks like a farce because it IS a farce.

Trump calls their bluff

It's been a two-month long farce in which Democratic leadership and DNC Media outlets gaslit the entire country by claiming the criminal leaker of the Ukraine phone call is some kind of heroic whistleblower and his name must be **protected**.

It's absurd that Schiff & Nadler pretended they don't know the leaker's name, and DNC media outlets pretend that PUBLISHING the name is A Very Bad Thing.

It's literally right out of Harry Potter! The criminal leaker of the Ukraine phone call has become "He Who Must Not Be Named!"

Recently, Trump called this stupid bluff by deliberately retweeting the tweet shown below, which many people tell me they can STILL see on his timeline:

[The president's retweet is not pictured here. Consult the source article found in the footnote to see it.]

So now, after months of making the absurd claim that saying that nobody can say this leaker's name, they HAVE to claim Trump just broke the law.

He called their bluff.

This means the Democratic leadership and the DNC Media have only two choices:

They have to raise or they have to fold.

The clock is now ticking ... which will they do?

Incidentally, they rose by sending articles of impeachment to the Senate. By the time you are reading this, we have all seen how the impeachment gambit played out. Spoiler alert: not well for Chairman Schiff and friends.

In keeping with Belloc's principle outlined in the chapter on fake news, it is a salutary practice to read a variety of sources, lest one run the risk of having your own biases and prejudices confirmed. A favorite writer of mine is a man named James Howard Kunstler. Reading him, for someone who loves good writing, is a visceral pleasure. I agree with him on some things and disagree on others. He writes on a variety of social topics, most famously on the enervating effects of suburbia and the long-term unsustainability of an economy predicated on cheap and abundant oil. But he is no radical green, and if I recall correctly, he has written about how many favorite sources of energy among the radical environmentalists are non-starters. He correctly identifies the only viable source if you want to move towards a low-carbon future: nuclear. But that is not germane to our discussion, and again one can disagree with him or agree as you see fit. But like the honest man that he is, he knows the depth of criminality to which the deep state has descended in recent years.

With regards to the impeachment fiasco, he kept a sort of running commentary at his blog which can be found at Kunstler.com. So, here is the witty and well-written perspective of James Howard Kunstler, no man of the right he, and his candid observations on the impeachment. His individual blog postings are titled and dated, so you can "get a feel" for the commentary as it ran. If you are not familiar with just what went on, I think this entertaining read will be enlightening.

JM

Impeachment-A-Rama,

or Part Two of a Coup,

**or ". . . from the Charlatans Who Brought You
Russia Gate Comes 'the Sequel' Ukraine Gate"**

Halloween Is Over and the Jig Is Up (Nov. 1, 2019)

And so Nancy Pelosi and Adam Schiff take the Republic into a dangerous defile on a dark day as they engineer a House resolution with rules for a medieval-style inquiry on the existence of phantoms. The phantom du jour, of course, is the fabled "whistleblower," a CIA ectoplasm identified by everybody and his uncle in Swampland as [a certain] former Joe Biden staffer, Obama White House low-level NSC holdover, and John Brennan "asset" deeply involved in Ukrainian pranks during the 2016 election and subsequent disinformation leakage to the media since the early days of the Trump administration. . . .

It seems obvious that the Democrats' mad rush to this wholly irregular impeachment happened in direct, proportional response to the encroaching danger to them posed by the DOJ inspector general's imminent report and the news a week ago that the AG upgraded his "review" of all things RussiaGate to a criminal inquiry, with grand juries assembled to process indictments. In the meantime, Rep. Schiff's secret proceedings in the House basement seem to have produced little besides evidence that contradicts the premises of his wicked enterprise. One by one, his witnesses have been busted . . . in Mr. Schiff's quixotic effort to demonstrate that the transcript of Mr. Trump's phone call to Mr. Zelensky says something other than what can be read plainly in its pages.

It's hard to feature how the House might convey their garbage barge of obvious falsehoods to the Senate — the risks are so perilous — but if they dare to, I hope it leads to an actual trial, where due process of law will obtain and, for the first time, a long list of malicious actors in this epic of treachery will actually have to answer for their treasonous activities. Much of what has been documented the past two years about the coup to oust Mr. Trump never made it to the pages of *The New York Times*, *WashPo*, and the cable news networks, and may come as a shock to people who read and watch nothing else. . . .[7]

The House of Representatives goes on hiatus now for about ten days. There's a pretty good chance the DOJ IG Horowitz's report will drop before they return. There's also more than a fair chance that it will contain a load of damning information about matters connected one way or another to the impeachment inquiry. I doubt the mainstream media will be able to evade reporting on it. There are also indications that the long ordeal of General Michael Flynn's prosecution is about to end in a debacle for Mr. Mueller's gang of attorneys, who have been concealing their turpitudes from Judge Emmet Sullivan's court since last December. When

---

[7]   Fake news narrative control and engineering, however, is in the process of being blown up as the name Durham, US Attorney, haunts the Swamp. Again, by the time you are reading these words, you may be following hearings and/or trials on TV. JM.

that case blows up, the reverberations will thunder through every cranny of Washington DC and everything on the battlefield will look changed to the people of this land.

The Deep State's Deep State Department (Nov. 15, 2019)

For now, it comes down to this: the US State Department is at war with the White House. State's allies in the Democratic majority congress want to help overthrow the occupant of the White House because he's *interfering* in the department's foreign policy. The lifers at State are the same ones who executed a coup in 2014 against Ukraine's government and threw out the elected president Victor Yanukovych because he tilted to join a Russian-backed regional customs union rather than NATO. State's diplomatic lifers are old hands at coups. Now they're at it at home, right here in the USA.

Ever since the Maidan Revolution of 2014, they have worked sedulously to exert control over Ukrainian affairs. And they especially can't stand that the recently elected president Zelensky declared that he wants to improve his country's relationship with next-door-neighbor (and ex-sovereign) Russia. The occupant of the White House, Mr. Trump, had often expressed a similar interest to improve the USA's relations with Russia. State would prefer to amp up a new cold war. Mr. Trump has some nerve *interfering* with that!

The lifers at State also have something to hide: their exertions to connive with Ukraine government officials they controlled to *interfere* in the 2016 US presidential election in favor of their former boss, Mrs. Clinton. The current impeachment spectacle is an attempt to pitch a smokescreen over that embarrassing mess, which includes the CIA's and FBI's efforts to blame Russia for their own illegal interventions in the 2016 election — the heart of the three-year impeachment narrative. The Joe-and-Hunter Biden affair is the left anterior descending artery in that heart.

The current testimony in the House Intel Committee raises another question. Whose back-channel diplomats are legitimate in US foreign policy: Mr. Trump's personal lawyer, Rudolph Giuliani, or State's own boy, billionaire freelance international political adventurer George Soros? The president dispatched Mr. Giuliani to Ukraine because he didn't trust the State lifers to get to the bottom of the mischief emanating from Kiev during the 2016 election, in which State lifers played an active role, along with Mr. Soros and his agents — in particular an outfit called the AntiCorruption Action Center, jointly funded by Mr. Soros and State (i.e. US taxpayers).

Mr. Soros's AntiCorruption Action Center was one entity that then US Ambassador Marie Yovanovitch submitted to Ukraine's then General Prosecutor Yuriy Lutsenko on a "do not investigate" list, according to reporter John Solomon. Solomon writes:

In other words, State was confirming its own embassy had engaged in pressure on Ukrainian prosecutors to drop certain law enforcement cases, just as Lutsenko and other Ukrainian officials had alleged.... More recently, George Kent, the embassy's charge d'affaires in 2016 and now a deputy assistant secretary of state, confirmed in impeachment testimony that he personally signed the April 2016 letter demanding Ukraine drop the case against the Anti-Corruption Action Centre.

Translation: an activist US embassy meddled in Ukraine's internal political affairs. That's a breach of international law. No doubt Marie Yovanovitch will be asked about these matters starting in about 15 minutes from as I write. Mr. Soros funded a network of nonprofits operating in Ukraine going back a decade, including the International Renaissance Foundation, the Open Society Foundation, Project Syndicate, and the CIA-connected Atlantic Council, which also received millions in support from Ukrainian gas pipe oligarch Victor Pinchuk. (Guess who else is a consort of the Atlantic Council — International Man of Mystery and 2016 election *meddler* Joseph Mifsud.) In 2015, Pinchuk paid $150,000 to Donald Trump's foundation for Mr. Trump to speak by video-link to a Kiev conference for strengthening Ukraine's ties to the West. At the same time, Pinchuk had contributed $25 million to the Clinton Foundation. [Ahh, the Clinton Foundation. JM]

Entertaining Questions (Nov. 18, 2019)

Anyone who doubts that the Attorney General is dead serious about cleaning up the . . . mess of sedition spawned by the Democratic Party, its agents in the permanent Washington bureaucracy, and its public relations arm in the news media, might invest a little time and attention in William Barr's speech to the Federalist Society Friday evening.

Mr. Barr declared unambiguously and in plain English that "in waging a scorched earth, no-holds-barred war of

'Resistance' against this Administration, it is the Left that is engaged in the systematic shredding of norms and the undermining of the rule of law." Is any part of that unclear? The confounded might take in this more detailed lesson in recent history from the speech:

"Immediately after President Trump won election, opponents inaugurated what they called 'the Resistance,' and they rallied around an explicit strategy of using every tool and maneuver available to sabotage the functioning of his administration. Now, 'resistance' is the language used to describe insurgency against rule imposed by an occupying military power. It obviously connotes that the government is not legitimate. This is a very dangerous — indeed incendiary — notion to import into the politics of a democratic republic. What it means is that, instead of viewing themselves as the "loyal opposition," as opposing parties have done in the past, they essentially see themselves as engaged in a war to cripple, by any means necessary, a duly elected government."

The Storms of December (Nov. 22, 2019)

Finally, you're left with that image of Adam Schiff sitting stock straight in the big chair with pursed lips and eyes bugged out, as in a very certain species of lunacy heretofore only seen in *Canis latrans* of Cartoon-land when, say, he has overrun the cliff's edge clutching an anvil to his bosom. What was he thinking when he hatched this latest quixotic chapter in the ignominious crusade to reverse the 2016 election?

That he'd never get caught? On Wednesday he witlessly did gave away the game on nationwide TV, telling the witness, heroic Col. Vindman, to not state which intel agency (of 23 !) employed the one still-unnamed person he blabbed to about the epic Phone Call to Ukraine — *because it would reveal the name of the "Whistleblower."* How could that be? Both Mr. Schiff and Col. Vindman claimed to not know the identity of the "WB?" If so, it would be logically impossible to reveal the "Whistleblower" by just naming an agency with thousands of little worker bees. Of course, he walked right into the trap set by minority member, Mr. Ratcliffe of Texas. Who doesn't get that Col Vindman knows exactly who the "Whistleblower" is because he was the "Whistleblower's" accomplice? And Mr. Schiff knows, too.

If the senate majority poohbahs were wise, they would warmly welcome a trial based on articles of impeachment, which would, of course, feature no artificial limits on the witness list, nor on questions that might be asked. The list might start with the UkraineGate "Whistleblower." Among the many untruths uttered by Adam Schiff was the nonexistent law that gave that shadowy figure a right to anonymity. And besides, in any trial based on due process, the accused has an absolute right to face his accuser.

The Resistance Digs Their Hole Deeper (Nov. 25, 2019)

The CIA, the FBI, the State Department have all been players in the coup to overthrow Mr. Trump and the news media played along the whole way. They doubled, tripled, and quadrupled down on their dishonest narrative and now they are trapped in it. They are desperate to evade responsibility for all this. Many people think they will succeed. Many people want to believe the story that Russia hacked the 2016 election to help Mr. Trump defeat Hillary. The story is not true. The perps are finally being found out. They are willing to bring the country down rather than face the consequences.

Death Wish (Dec. 2, 2019)

Really, the only question now is what new way will Mr. Nadler find to humiliate himself and mortify his party? Opening testimony this week will be supplied by a panel of Woke constitutional law professors who will attempt to tease out some hermeneutic legal basis for an impeachment other than actual misdeeds. They'll surely settle on thought-crime, since there is nothing else. Whose idea was it to hit the snooze button just as the curtain goes up on the show?

Next will come a mighty hassle over whether the minority can call witnesses of its own choosing. Ranking member Doug Collins (R-GA) has already asked for an appearance by Adam Schiff, chair of the House Intel Committee, whose procedural shenanigans last month embarrassed anyone with a vestigial memory of Anglo-American due process. Some folks think that Mr. Schiff has got some 'splainin' to do about the predicating circumstances of his star chamber spectacle. He is, in fact, a fact-witness to all that, on top of being the issuer today of his own committee's report on all that, and therefore susceptible to public examination — especially in a train of proceedings as grave as impeachment. If Mr. Nadler enables Mr. Schiff to slither out of testifying, there will be hell to pay, and in the not-so-likely prospect of an actual impeachment trial in the senate, it would be paid there as an unleashed defense goes for Mr. Schiff with pithing needles and thumbscrews of genuine interrogation.

Then there is the "Whistleblower," this would-be pimpernel of perfidy hiding behind Adam Schiff's apron under the false assertion that he is entitled to everlasting anonymity. What an idea under our system of jurisprudence! In fact, contrary to Mr. Schiff's public pronouncements, there is no law that states what he claims — one of several things Mr. Schiff can be called to account for. And that is even if you accept the dishonest proposition that the fugitive who started this fiasco even *was* a whistleblower, rather than a rogue CIA officer acting on explicitly illegal political motives to *interfere in the 2020 election.* The CIA, you must know, is forbidden by charter and statute from operating against American citizens in-country, including the president of the United States. Under the circumstances, the so-called "Whistleblower" might fairly be accused of treason.

Has anyone failed to notice that one of the "Whistleblower's" attorneys, Mark Zaid, tweeted notoriously on January 30, 2017 that "***Coup has started. First of many steps. #rebellion. #impeachment will follow ultimately. #lawyers.***" Mr. Zaid later explained, "I was referring to a completely lawful process." Yeah, sure. . . . Of course, the engineered "Whistleblower" escapade was only the latest (perhaps the last) chapter in the annals of nefarious events and actions carried out far-and-wide by several government agencies for three years, and by many officials working within them, and not a few freelance rogues in their service. There is no more accurate way to describe all that except as a coup. The authorities looking into *all that* have not been heard from yet. The portentous silence is making a lot of people in Washington edgy.

If the various House committees have put the Democratic Party on suicide watch, then something even more deadly is lurking just offstage. Hillary Clinton is making noises about jumping into the 2020 election. She senses opportunity as Joe Biden goes pitifully through the motions of running for office to avoid prosecution for his international grifting operations as Veep. Think of Hillary as the cyanide capsule that the party might actually choose to bite down on as the year ominously turns.

The War of the Narratives (Dec. 9, 2019)

Fighting for its very life, the Resistance rolls out a last-ditch flanking maneuver today in its three-year war against reality as Rep. Adam Schiff's House Intel Committee presents findings to Rep. Nadler's Judiciary Committee for crimes as yet unspecified against Mr. Trump, possibly as grave as treason. Buyer beware. The Resistance always accuses its enemy of the very acts it commits — for instance, colluding with Russia, the primal deed that the guiding spirit of the Resistance, Mrs. Clinton, perpetrated in hiring Glenn Simpson's Fusion GPS outfit and its star front-man, Christopher Steele, to consort with Russian disinformation agents injecting some helpful fantasy into the 2016 election.

Therefore, you can be serenely confident that any charges of actual treason will eventually stick to members of Resistance in government service who did indeed plot a coup to overthrow the occupant of the White House. That process of discovery begins today in another part of the battlefield, when the DOJ Inspector General, Mr. Horowitz, rolls out his report on FISA court shenanigans. His inquiry, of course, was limited to current members of the DOJ and FBI, which leaves out many of the principal actors in that scheme . . . — all either discharged or moved onto other thickets in the reeking wetland of Washington DC. Anyway, the coup ranged far beyond the bounds of Mr. Horowitz's scope on FISA abuse.

Among those many others, the IG was not authorized to interrogate former CIA chief John Brennan, the Lone Ranger of RussiaGate, or James Clapper, former Director of National Intelligence, Mr. Brennan's faithful Tonto in the scam. . . .

One character who has not been heard from lo these many months is former associate deputy attorney general Bruce Ohr, who was *not* fired, but transferred to some harmless backwater of the Justice Department to answer agency parking violations, or something equally harmless. I suspect Mr. Ohr may have played a decisive role in the IG inquiry, and possibly flipped on his colleagues, since Mr. Ohr was in the uniquely uncomfortable position of having a wife, Nellie Ohr, in the direct employ of Fusion GPS, Hillary Clinton's oppo research contractor. Mr. Ohr additionally consorted with Fusion's front man, Mr. Steele, after Steele was officially fired as a paid FBI source. Mr. Ohr will surely play a role on the Durham side of things. . . .

So, you see, we have two narratives at war in America: the Resistance story aimed at shoving Mr. Trump out of the White House by any means necessary, including a siege engine of untruth based on bad faith; and Mr. Trump's story that he has been unfairly and unjustly subject to seditious mutiny by several federal agencies, dedicated to crippling his executive function at least and levering him out of office at most. The two stories can be reconciled in courts of law and the court of public opinion. There's polling evidence that the Resistance is losing in the latter, as it over-estimated the public's appetite for official dishonesty. The courts of law await further down the road.

Two for One Holiday Special (Dec. 13, 2019)

Hillary Clinton sure got her money's worth with the Fusion GPS deal: it induced a three-year psychotic break in the body politic, destroyed the legitimacy of federal law enforcement, turned a once-proud, free, and rational press into an infernal engine of bad faith, and is finally leading her Democratic Party to an ignominious suicide. And the damage is far from complete. It's even possible that Mrs. Clinton will return to personally escort the party over the cliff when, as is rumored lately, she jumps into the primary contest and snatches the gonfalon of leadership from the ailing old man of the sclerotic status quo, Uncle Joe Biden.

The citizens of this foundering polity have been subjected to a stunning doubleheader of political spectacle clear through the week. On Monday, the Horowitz Report was briefly celebrated by the Left for claiming "no bias" and a "reasonable predicate" for the RussiaGate mess — until auditors actually got to read the 400-plus-page document and discovered that it was absolutely stuffed with incriminating details that Mr. Horowitz was too polite, too coy, or too faint-hearted to identify as acts worthy of referral for prosecution.[8]

Mr. Barr, the attorney general, and US attorney John Durham immediately stepped up to set the record straight, namely, that this was hardly the end of the matter and that they were privy to fact-trains of evidence that would lead, by-and-by, to a quite different conclusion. This reality-test was greeted, of course, with shrieking for their dismissal from the Jacobin Left. But then at mid-week, Mr. Horowitz put in a personal appearance before the Senate Judiciary Committee and left no doubt that entire RussiaGate extravaganza was spawned by Fusion GPS's utterly false Steele dossier and the so-called "Intel Community's" zeal for weaponizing it to overthrow the president.

The shock-waves from all that still pulsate through the disordered collective consciousness of this sore-beset republic, and will disturb the sleep of many former and current officials for months to come as the specter of Barr & Durham transmutes into a nightmare of Hammer & Tongs, perp-walks, and actual prosecutions. . . .

All the week long, the Horowitz Report and its aftershocks were attended by the impeachment show in Jerrold

---

[8] I may be reading between the lines a bit too much here, but during his testimony before Congress, Inspector General Horowitz, when asked by Sen. Joni Ernst (R-IA) why he did not make any criminal referrals, seemed to me to say that the entire report constituted a referral and so that was what they sent. Inspector General Report on Origins of FBI's Russia Inquiry, C-SPAN, video, 00:46, December 11, 2019, https://www.c-span.org/video/?c4838137/user-clip-ernst-horowitz-criminal-referrals. JM

Nadler's House Judiciary Committee — an exercise so devoid of sense and prudence that it would embarrass all the kangaroos ever assembled in the courts of legend.

An Expulsion of Demons (Dec. 16, 2019)

How much ignominy can they endure? Have they not grasped the reality that the Mueller investigation failed? That it appears to have been only one part of a larger criminal enterprise to defraud the public? That the Resistance was just an effort to cover up swales of wickedness in a greater swamp of government-gone-rogue? And now, to come to this: two articles of impeachment so transparently empty that they look like windows into the vacated soul of the Democratic Party.

And now consider all this vectoring into the catastrophe that the Democratic primary has become heading into election 2020. Joe Biden? Really? Are they serious? He left a slime trail as wide as the DC Beltway around his doings as Veep, with enough video evidence to make the College of Cardinals weep for his post-mortal prospects. Elizabeth Warren and Bernie Sanders might be moved to study up on what just happened in the UK election, and weigh how US voters might be disposed to another four-year beat-down with the cudgels of *inclusion* and *diversity* plus the shady blandishments of free everything. . . .

This solemn holiday may be the Democrat Party's last chance to avoid suicide. They need to have a conversation with someone on the cosmic hotline, come to the realization that they've truly hit bottom now and must, as Rep Devin

Nunes suggested Sunday to his colleague Adam Schiff, sign into rehab.

Grave Tendings (Jan. 17, 2020)

So titanically self-unaware is the Democratic Resistance that it failed to grok[9] it was actually signing the party's death warrant Wednesday, complete with official Nancy Pelosi commemorative black-and-gold signature pens. And that their *solemn, prayerful* journey from one side of the Capitol building to the other was actually the conveyance of that death warrant in what amounted to the party's funeral march. Remember this eternal paradox of the human condition: *people get what they deserve, not what they expect. . . .*

Could they actually be so dim as to proffer "abuse of power" and "obstruction of congress" as articles of impeachment? These two figments would be laughed out of a second-year law school mock court. Legal necromancers of the future, with all the time in the world, may never unpack the intended meaning of these charges besides "we hate you" and "you hurt our feelings." But it's up to the Senate of today to dispose of them procedurally one way or another, and the exercise is sure to be a high order of entertainment.

In a sane world of rational adults, these charges would be cooly dismissed out-of-hand as lacking any discernible malfeasant substance. As we live in a time of hysteria, the normal rules don't apply. That being the case, the defense should spare no mercy in unmasking the bad faith and fraud

---

9   "to understand or get," Ed.

on offer by doing what the House Democrats have asked for, calling witnesses, so as to walk the Democrats into the fiery furnace of humiliation and infamy they so richly deserve. . . .

What would soon be obvious is that the precipitating "whistleblower" caper was an effort to divert attention from a network of Americans that used a politically captive Ukraine — following the Maidan Revolution of 2014 — to protect an enormous racketeering operation threatened by the candidacy, and then the election, of Mr. Trump. Naturally, they are desperate to get him out of the way. So many of the facts are already publicly known and documented about these matters that the legal machinery has yet to catch up with it all. And when it does, the Democratic Party will have driven a wooden stake through its own depraved heart.

Funeral Arrangements (Jan. 20, 2020)

As they like to say in the horror movie trailers: *It… begins…!* (Cue bassoons and waterphones.)

If last Wednesday's *solemn and prayerful* parade through the Capitol rotunda was the Democratic Party's funeral march, then impeachment starting this week may be the burial service. Central casting couldn't have found a more perfect funeral director than the grave and genteel Mitch McConnell. . . .

And, naturally, the witness question beats a path directly to the Bidens. Open that door and there is really nothing on God's green earth that will keep Hunter B out of the witness chair. In which case he will have to reiterate what he said in a TV interview a few months back — they'll play the recording in-session — which is that he got the $83-K-a-month do-nothing gig on the Burisma board-of-directors because he was the Vice-president's son. Or he can change his story and cast himself as a liar. It would not be necessary to call Joe Biden, just submit in evidence that recording of him bragging on how he strong-armed the Ukrainians to shut down their Burisma investigation by threatening to withhold a billion-dollar aid-and-loan package. Hmmmm. Sounds suspiciously like what Mr. Trump is accused of, absent evidence.

Was Jerrold Nadler (D-NY) playing dumb on *Face the Nation* Sunday when he said Hunter Biden shouldn't testify because he has no knowledge of the accusation? Or, is Mr. Nadler just dumb enough to forget that in a trial, the person accused of something is called *the defendant* because he's entitled to defend himself? The corruption in the Hunter B matter is not just obvious, it's confessed. Everyone seems to have forgotten that the US has a treaty with Ukraine on mutual legal assistance in criminal matters signed at Kiev on July 22, 1998. How, exactly, does that *not* apply to Mr. Trump's conversation with Mr. Zelensky?

Well, all this tends, naturally, to questions around the 2020 election. . . .

Bernie Sanders looked to be coming on strong in recent weeks, until Project Veritas caught some of his field managers threatening to burn down Milwaukee if he was deprived of the nomination and then proceed with a national insurrection. Was that a true colors moment? Voters have a right to wonder if Bernie is piloting a garbage barge of old-time Bolshevism, complete with the requisite reign of terror.

Just today *The New York Times* endorsed Elizabeth Warren and Amy Klobuchar for president. Yes, you probably thought what I thought initially: one for Prez, one for Veep. Actually, no, it was both for Prez. How's that supposed to work? Well, it's just a ruse, of course, because both are foundering in the polls, and poor Ms. Warren is on tape lying about herself so many times that you'd see more of that on TV than *Seinfeld* reruns before next November. *The New York Times* is actually holding out for the resurrection of Hillary Clinton. Isn't this the perfect set-up for old Hillary to swoop into Milwaukee on her leathery wings of fire, like the fearsome Wendigo of Potawatomi legend, and gobble up the delegates? It would be much like the Whigs nominating the old warhorse General Winfield Scott in the election of 1852. That election marked the death of the Whig Party, and with Hillary leading the charge, 2020 would be the end of the Democrats, such as they were known.

The impeachment witness question also redounds upon the fabled "whistleblower," that Jacob Marley of the impeachment Christmas story, rattling his chains off-stage and wailing of cosmic injustice against the poor Ukrainians. There is no witness more pertinent to this enormous fiasco than that pimpernel of perfidy — and, of course, the long choo-choo train of persons he conspired with, including Adam Schiff and the Lawfare gang. I would love to see him unmasked in the 'splainin' seat, spilling the beans on the predication of this whole sordid affair. But it might be better to wait and hear from him in the Senate Judiciary Committee hearings to follow this impeachment circus, where his turpitudes can get the full attention they deserve, with indictments to follow.

The Big Sleep (Jan. 24, 2020)

Those who were only puzzling over Nancy Pelosi's motives in bringing this case, and assigning it to the two sketchiest characters in her charge, Schiff & Nadler, must finally be convinced that she is no longer sound of mind. What was she thinking? Did she really want to set up the voters to lose faith in the basic electoral process by preemptively delegitimizing the 2020 election? (*"Trump can only win if he cheats!"*) Is she that desperate to flip the Senate to prevent anymore judicial appointments? Could be. Or is the impeachment spectacle a different kind of set-up: to make the forthcoming raft of indictments against RussiaGate coupsters look like a mere act of revenge rather than long-delayed justice for a three-year campaign of perfidious sedition by some of the highest officials in the land?

Anyway, after another day of this boresome torment, the Senate will get to hear Mr. Trump's defense in a full-throated way — really for the first time since the whole nasty business began, and in a conspicuous venue where it can't be ignored anymore. If nothing else, it will probably be more interesting and certainly more dignified than the idiotic vaudeville put on by Schiff & Nadler. Even if the President's managers move to dismiss the case out-of-hand for its utter lack of merit and the legal errors in its construction by two House committees, I doubt they will miss the opportunity to use the time allotted to lay out the story of what actually happened the past three years — a crime spree of government against itself. . . .

In the meantime, an interesting development flew in under the radar as the impeachment spectacle hogged the news: The Department of Justice yesterday declared two of four FISA warrants against Carter Page invalid. The warrants were signed by James Comey, Andrew McCabe, and Rod Rosenstein. The move has deep repercussions in everything connected to the RussiaGate investigation, including especially the prosecutions mounted by Robert Mueller's lawyers. It implies what has already been demonstrated by other evidence: That the FBI and the DOJ knew by January of 2017 at the latest that all the information they used to start the case against the President was garbage, and yet they continued it anyway — including the appointment of Mr. Mueller and his commission. The DOJ's statement about the two FISA warrants doesn't negate the possibility that the other two will also be declared invalid. It's time for the figures involved in all this to become very afraid.

Tales from the Crypt (Jan. 31, 2020)

What a fatal mistake, allowing Rep. Adam Schiff (D-CA) to make himself the face of the Democratic Party. They would have been better off with another scion of Hollywood: the Phantom of the Opera. This grubby seditionist has marched the party into a wilderness of deceit and knavery that taints them all, and when this grotesque impeachment episode is over, a new chapter of consequences will open that should leave the party for dead.

. . . A universe of chaos lurks behind Mr. Schiff's slick Tinseltown façade. The impeachment he led was crippled from the start with violations of process and errors of logic of exactly the kind that drives his party's Woke hysteria with its assaults on free speech, its vicious "cancel" culture, its reckless race-hatred, its depraved Transsexual Reading Hours, and its neurotic obsession with Russian phantoms — a matrix of beliefs that would embarrass a conclave of medieval necromancers.

Of course, the impeachment was just the latest sortie in a three-year campaign to confound and conceal the arrant misdeeds of a network of government employees in the Departments of State and Justice, the FBI, the CIA, and the remnants of Barack Obama's White House, who are all connected and all liable for prosecution . . . .

The "Whistleblower" in the current impeachment fiasco was a CIA agent and John Brennan protégé who had worked for Joe Biden both in the US and on trips to Ukraine when he was detailed to the Obama White House. Hunter Biden was known to be a dangerous abscess of grift years before Mr. Trump ever rode down that fabled golden escalator, and the "WB" was present for White House meetings with Ukrainian officials when embarrassing questions about Burisma and the Bidens came up. His supposed right to anonymity is fairytale and the time is not far off when he'll have to answer for his deeds, whether it's in a Senate committee or a grand jury.

The Intel Inspector General who ushered him into the spotlight, Michael Atkinson, was chief counsel to the same DOJ officials who signed phony FISA warrants and who ramped up both the dishonest "Crossfire Hurricane" scam and its two-year continuation as the Mueller Special Counsel investigation. All of this activity involved the same gang of top FBI officials, DOJ lawyers, and Lawfare intriguers. It has obviously been a broad attempt to overthrow a president by any means, including plenty of collusion with foreign governments. In a truly just society, this ring would be busted under federal RICO and conspiracy raps, and perhaps they will be.

You can see the next installment taking shape through the last stages of the impeachment fog. Both Speaker Nancy Pelosi and Senate Minority Leader "Chuck" Schumer have declared that "acquittal is meaningless." Somebody ought to inform them that the hole they want to keep digging is the Democratic Party's grave. Can there be no Democrats who are nauseated by what has gone down in their name, who understand the damage that has been wreaked by their own leaders, who are sick of re-investing in falsehoods and perfidy? . . .

As to the election of 2020, the Democrats are trying like hell to set the stage for disputing and negating it. In fact, that has mostly been the hidden agenda behind this hot mess of an impeachment. They will at least attempt to litigate it into a dangerous state of irresolution. Wouldn't that be grand?

Yes, Virginia, there was a coup attempt in the United States, in multiple stages, and the impeachment was part of it. Who would have thunk it? But honest people from the Left, Right, and Center, people not locked into the "respectable news outlets"—that is, the fake news—have known about it for some time now. Today, the day after President Trump's acquittal in the Senate impeachment trial, having just watched his sort of celebratory speech in the White House, I think it is a safe bet that those Americans still unaware of what went on are in for a rude awakening in the coming months, leading up to November. And, contra the lie that the anti-Trump media was peddling immediately after the speech today, it will have nothing to do with vengeance and everything to do with justice carried out by the proper authorities. Buy popcorn stocks. Redenbacher shares are going to go through the roof.

JM

CONCLUSION

The Man With the Very Virtues We Need

*I would rather a boy learnt in the roughest school the
courage to hit a politician, or gained in the hardest school
the learning to refute him – rather than that he should gain
in the most enlightened school the cunning to copy him.*[1]

G. K. Chesterton

G. K. Chesterton could have been describing Donald Trump
when he penned those words. Donald Trump learned to hit,
to counterpunch as he says, in some of the roughest arenas
around: the New York City real estate, construction, and
political worlds. In other words, he's been through the school
of hard knocks where all three intersect. He also obtained,
again in some of the hardest schools—his high school military academy and the Wharton School of Business—the
formal education to be able to go toe-to-toe with his advisors, whether military, economic, or political, and be able to
give as good as he gets. Perhaps more than any politician in
American history, Donald Trump has the courage to "hit"
deserving politicians—and rarely have there been so many
truly deserving of such treatment—or to debate policy with

---

[1] "Quotations of G. K. Chesterton," *The Apostolate of Common
Sense*, https://www.chesterton.org/quotations-of-g-k-chesterton/.

197

them on the national stage or in the backrooms just off the corridors of power.

If you have read this far, it is our hope that the preceding chapters—and videos, if you have watched any—have convinced you that Donald Trump is the man to vote for in 2020.

As Catholics, we should look to our Church's authentic teachings to guide us and instruct us, especially when difficult moral questions arise. The election of 2020, however, does not present a difficult moral question. No true Catholic, in good conscience, should be able to vote for one of the Democrat candidates, all of whom support virtually, if not absolutely, unlimited abortion, the marginalization of religious freedom in the name of a misguided view of equality, and the craziness of the trans-rights movement. Many, in fact, support a political system, socialism, or some variant thereof, that has been explicitly condemned without qualification by multiple popes, and those who do not have nowhere demonstrated the vision and courage that Trump has in resetting the entire international framework of trade and commerce, a resetting that will allow America to stop bleeding good-paying jobs through a corrupt system that enriches a small international "elite" at the expense of the American working class.

Had Hillary Clinton won the 2016 election, Catholic life in this country would have been circumscribed. Happily, she did not. Sadly, it seems that for the foreseeable future, if any Democrat attains the highest political office in the land, as their party is currently constituted, Catholic life and freedom will be circumscribed in the name of diversity and a twisted kind of "tolerance." The differences between the Democrat candidates in that regard will only affect how slowly or quickly that occurs, not whether it does. In short, they won't let us be Catholic; they don't want to let Catholic schools be Catholic, Catholic nuns be Catholic, Catholic adoption agencies be Catholic. On an individual level, perhaps some would, but the powers that be behind the Democrats today and the whole drift of the culture they support is hostile to the faith and our practice of it. Just ask Father Pavone or the Little Sisters of the Poor. Donald Trump, on the other hand, is an ally. Corey Lewandowski and David Bossie wrote a book called *Letting Trump Be Trump.* Trump will let Catholics be Catholic. Compared to the Democrat candidates, their platform, and desired policies, that counts for a lot.

But what of the man himself? Some Catholics will tell you they vote for the man despite his character. They are wrong. You should vote for him precisely *because of* his character, for only a man of his character, warts and all, could have taken on the corrupt establishment and won. Donald Trump is a leader of men, but more than that, he is a virtuous man, granted imperfectly so, but aren't we all (cf. Rom 3:23)?

The seven virtues we Catholics most often talk about can be divided into two groups: the cardinal virtues of prudence, justice, temperance, and fortitude and the theological virtues of faith, hope, and love.

We would like to conclude by looking at the man in the light of the cardinal virtues. It would be folly to try to do so in every area of his life. To paraphrase Pope Francis, "Who

are we to judge?" Rather, we will do so with regard to his role
as candidate and president.

Prudence

"Prudence disposes the practical reason to discern, in every
circumstance, our true good and to choose the right means
of achieving it."[2]

Donald Trump is a prudent man. He discerned the right
time for a run at the presidency. Defying the experts and
received DC wisdom, he pulled off the greatest political upset in modern history. He seems to have remarkable
instincts, if not in every, then certainly in most circumstances. He knows our true good is to bring back manufacturing and that the lies of the neoliberal economic globalist
"free" traders were just that: lies (well, lies for some, misguided errors for others) designed to enrich a global elite at
the expense of the middle and lower class in this country.
In foreign policy, he knows who our number one enemy is,
and it ain't Russia. It is radical Islamic terrorism, and he has
forged remarkable coalitions in the Middle East designed to
destroy it, root and branch, after his predecessors fostered
its growth and expansion. In his battle against the swamp,
the deep state, and the resistance, he has let things unfold
slowly, too slowly for many, and he undoubtedly is making
concessions along the way, but increasingly it seems that his
approach has been the right one. Brian Cates writes about
this often. Many of Trump's most ardent supporters seem to

---

[2]   CCC 1835.

think that he is incompetent in his hires and that if only he had listened to them and blown up the deep state on Day 1 of his presidency, everything would be fine. But he did not. Most likely had he done so, it would have caused tremendous turmoil and upheaval. As his attorney general William Barr quipped in one interview, "These things take time." Trump is not perfect, and no one agrees with the prudential judgment of anyone else 100 percent of the time, but Donald Trump is a prudent man. And where he may be viewed as imprudent, we will take his unique brand of courage any day of the week: a case in point is his being the first president to address the March for Life "live," first remotely and then, this year, in person. We are sure some of his advisors told him not to, that it would be "imprudent." We like Trump's courage of his convictions.

Justice

"Justice consists in the firm and constant will to give God and neighbor their due."[3]

"Because you'd be in jail." That line is perhaps the most prominent example of his commitment to justice and the one for which he will be most remembered. But there are many others, including his freeing of numerous prisoners who have been in jail for too long and have been rehabilitated or were unjustly jailed in the first place, his desire to return a decent standard of living to the American working class, his desire for trade deals that are truly fair and free, his

---

[3]   CCC 1836.

carving out space for religious entities, families, and individuals to carry out their mission and live their lives unimpeded by a rabidly secularist vision of society and the United States Constitution (which is not in keeping with that Constitution by the way).

Though it is difficult to pin down with any degree of certitude Donald Trump's religious views, one can only surmise that to have gone through what he has since he announced his campaign and throughout his presidency, he has had to rely on God perhaps more than ever before in his life. The fact that he does not wear his religion on his sleeve is not something we hold against him. At the same time, his speech at the March for Life seemed, like all of Trump's speeches, authentic and sincere. And he spoke unapologetically and very comfortably about God, the dignity of human life and the soul. Consider: "All of us here today understand an eternal truth: Every child is a precious and sacred gift from God. Together, we must protect, cherish, and defend the dignity and sanctity of every human life. When we see the image of a baby in the womb, we glimpse the majesty of God's creation. When we hold a newborn in our arms, we know the endless love that each child brings to a family. When we watch a child grow, we see the splendor that radiates from each human soul."[4]

Sounds like one of us, doesn't he?

---

[4] Donald Trump, "Remarks by President Trump at the 47th Annual March for Life," The White House, January 24, 2020, https://www.whitehouse.gov/briefings-statements/remarks-president-trump-47th-annual-march-life/.

Temperance

"Temperance moderates the attractions of the pleasures of the senses and provides balance in the use of created goods."[5]

Well, this may seem a tougher nut than the others given Trump's brash persona and embrace of and flaunting of his personal wealth, but is it? It was mentioned that Trump was a man about town in years past, but one who was temperate, nay, abstemious when it came to alcohol and drugs. He has never indulged in either. That said, he is certainly intemperate in his criticism of his enemies, and we don't say political enemies, for the noun needs no modifier. This is a war we are witnessing between Donald Trump and the establishment—some of the members of which with their very freedom on the line—and the stakes are high. Yes, Trump is intemperate in his attacks on them, but he has every right to be mad. He is intemperate against them because he loves America and Americans so much, and they have undoubtedly committed high crimes. So, let's see what happens and whether President Trump was wrong to be intemperate. Something tells us he will, in fact, be revealed to have exercised a fair amount of restraint once the full story is told of just who violated the laws of these United States and how, in their quest to prevent his victory in 2016 and then to remove him from office once he was inaugurated, they went about it. For our part, we eagerly look forward to hearing more from Mr. Durham.

---

[5] CCC 1838.

Fortitude

"Fortitude ensures firmness in difficulties and constancy in the pursuit of the good."[6]

If there be one virtue he seems to possess in spades, it would be this one. Donald Trump is a man of fortitude. Who else could have withstood all the attacks and lies that the media, the Democrats, and the Never Trump Republicans have directed against him since before his election? Who else, once in office, could have sustained and carried on in the face of widespread felonious leaking and treachery by deep state holdovers and plants in his own administration? Undoubtedly, President Trump and his family must be the target of even worse threats and menaces, the details of which we may never know. In a very real sense, Donald John Trump has given the country an object lesson in what it means to be a man of fortitude. As Catholics, we can hope that our bishops are watching and that the good ones will learn from him in that regard.

Incidentally, the Church in this country has an outstanding example of a bishop who fought for his flock in a way perhaps not all that dissimilar from the way in which the forty-fifth president fights for his people. As a New Yorker, it is expected that President Trump might like the story about Archbishop John "Dagger" Hughes.

---

[6]   CCC 1837.

"Dagger" and "the Donald"

In an article attributed to a Sister Elizabeth Ann, SJW, the most famous incident of Archbishop John "Dagger" Hughes's remarkable episcopate in New York is recounted. Sister writes:

> Hughes' third and most dangerous battle occurred in 1844, when anti-Catholic rioters in Philadelphia planned to come to New York. During the riots in Philadelphia, two Catholic churches had been burned down and twelve people had died. In response to this threat, Hughes put armed guards around the Catholic churches. Then Hughes warned the mayor that "if a single Catholic Church were burned in New York, the city would become a second Moscow." (The city of Moscow was burned to the ground by its own citizens to prevent Napoleon from using the city as winter quarters for his army.) Whether Hughes meant what he said or not will never be known. His threat was taken seriously enough for city leaders to force the rioters to cancel their rally. After these battles Hughes became "the best known, if not exactly the best-loved Catholic bishop in the country."[7]

There is, apparently, some question as to whether the incident detailed above is apocryphal; we hope not and believe not. It certainly sounds plausible given what we know of Archbishop Hughes. If not true, it should be. There are also

---

[7]   Sister Elizabeth Ann, "'Dagger John' (1797-1864)," Catholic Heritage Curricula, accessed February 27, 2020, https://www.chcweb.com/catalog/files/daggerjohn.pdf.

various versions of the story as to whether he used the threat about Moscow or other words to similar effect. It does not matter much; the point is clear. In another article, a review of a biography of the archbishop which appeared in *America* magazine, Reverend Anthony Andreassi concludes with the following passage.

> Hughes had the descriptor "Dagger" placed before his name in his own day (and ever since) due to his fiery personality, which blazed at times at those both within the church and without. In more recent years, some have criticized him for his bluster and street-fighter tactics. . . . However, in 1966 John Tracy Ellis offered a more nuanced (and arguably more valid) assessment of Hughes and his style of leadership. The former dean of U.S. Catholic history pointed out that American Protestantism of the 19th century was by no means as open and irenic as it has been for the last half-century. For this reason, according to Ellis, "there were times when [Hughes's] very aggressiveness was about the only approach that would serve the end he was seeking, viz., justice for his people."[8]

The "more nuanced (and arguably more valid) assessment of Hughes and his style of leadership" by Ellis, alluded to by Fr. Andreassi, could also be applied to President Trump and his style/tactics/bluster—call it what you will—that has so

---

[8]   Anthony D. Andreassi, "An archbishop nicknamed 'Dagger John,'" *America*, March 15, 2018, https://www.americamagazine .org/arts-culture/2018/03/15/archbishop-nicknamed-dagger -john.

offended so many, including many of our Catholic leaders, both clergy and lay. Donald Trump stands up for us in a way that precious few of our leaders have; Donald Trump fights for us, at great personal cost, in a way that precious few of our leaders have; Donald Trump has laid down his life of wealth for us in a way that certainly no politician has—for most of them become wealthy during and after their political careers rather than before, as he did.

Yes, Donald Trump has gone to war for us. "There were times when [Hughes's] very aggressiveness was about the only approach that would serve the end he was seeking, viz., justice for his people." Perhaps if, over the past fifty years, the Catholic Church in the United States had had a few men with the fortitude, courage, thirst for justice and, yes, perhaps even those qualities which many consider flaws of a Dagger Hughes, or, dare we say it, a Donald Trump, the country and our Church would be in a very different place today. It is our loss that we did not.

Faith, Hope, and Love

We will leave this look at the virtues of Donald Trump at the four cardinal ones; the three theological virtues seem to be somehow more personal. But we will note that the president has fought the good fight for the people who elected him. When all is said and done, President Trump, if he succeeds in his struggle against the corrupt establishment, will have done much to restore the average citizen's faith in his government; he already has done much to instill hope in millions around the country who had none, hope for the future and the future of their children, and he has loved his people, who in turn have loved him. Looking from afar, it seems to us that he strives to love God and hope in him and love him in his own imperfect way. But more importantly in his role as president, he will fight to the death to allow us Catholics to live out our lives of faith and hope and love in a free society.

May God bless Donald John Trump.

AFTERWORD

THIS book is scheduled to be released on March 17, 2020, which, as everyone knows, is St. Patrick's Day. It is difficult to think of a more appropriate day for its release than the feast day of that holy man who drove the snakes out of Ireland. For Donald Trump is driving the snakes out of Washington, DC.

It is a challenge to keep up with the news cycle, especially for a book publisher in this age of blogs, tweets, and twenty-four-hour news, especially during this administration when President Trump's accomplishments seem to come in such rapid succession, and especially during campaign season when the shape of the Democratic primary has changed dramatically in the last week.

What a surprise that Joe Biden is emerging as the choice of the Donkey Party! Apparently, the powers that be know that socialism is best rolled out more slowly than Bernie and his bros would like. Again, we would not want to own a three-bedroom in downtown Milwaukee this summer.

But for all their noise about diversity and inclusion, come November, it seems that the Democrats will put forth one of two old white men, "not that there's anything wrong with that." It's just that it seems to violate their shouted principles a tad.

If this is the best that the Democrats can do to challenge

Donald Trump, one does fear for the future of the party, that is if you have any affection for them. One suspects they have always known they stand no chance against the president at the ballot box and so will have to beat him by other means. It seems that the latest gambit is to lay the coronavirus at his feet. That is amazing and unfair, but par for the course for the fake news. Having seen the bird flu, swine flu, and other potential pandemics come and go, we wonder if the fear-mongering is a bit overdone, but time will tell.

Either way, we are confident that we would want nobody other than Donald John Trump in the White House during a difficult time. For it is not only through his successes that you gauge the mettle of a man or the merit of a president. No, quite often you can take the measure of a man much more accurately by observing him during the trials and vicissitudes of life.

On either metric, judged by his successes or how he handles adversity, Donald Trump is a man and president to be admired, even marveled at. Before and throughout his presidency, his opponents have stopped at nothing in their efforts to destroy him, but he soldiers on, doing great things for the country, with his good humor intact. If you doubt that, we refer you again to appendix 2.

His handling of events during the various weather-related disasters that have struck during his first term has been a case study in servant leadership. The media might not acknowledge that fact, but those affected by the tragedies whom he and Melania have visited know the truth, as does the rest of the country.

Donald Trump has weathered storms of all types, which

reminds us of a 2017 photo op[1] with a number of members of the military and their spouses. There, he asked the assembled media, "Do you guys know what this represents? . . . Could be the calm before the storm."

When asked what he meant by that, he said cryptically, "You'll find out."

There has been much speculation in certain corners of the internet as to just what storm the president was referring. Given the presence of the military, did it refer to offensives against ISIS or did it refer to something else, swamp-draining perhaps?

As has been hinted at and stated elsewhere throughout this book, it is our belief that the Obama/Biden/Clinton administration was one of, if not the most thoroughly corrupt administrations in American history. That is why, for those who may be wondering, we included the details of the Clinton email scandal; both to demonstrate the corruption that Trump had to root out as well as to highlight the importance of him winning a second term. That job is not done; in many ways it is not yet begun. We trust that between now and the election, the American people will learn much more about just how corrupt our government had become.

Our confidence that this will happen has been buoyed by a recent tweet by presidential assistant and director of social media at the White House Dan Scavino and its subsequent retweet by President Trump. On March 8, Scavino tweeted out the following with an image of President Trump playing

---

[1] "Donald Trump warns it is 'the calm before the storm,'" *The Telegraph*, video, 0:38, October 6, 2017, https://www.youtube.com/watch?v=HH0AvaG3SqQ.

the violin: "My next piece is called . . . Nothing can stop what's coming."

Later that day, the president retweeted it and wrote, "Who knows what this means? But it sounds good to me!"

It sounds good to us as well, Mr. President, and we have confidence that you, at least, know exactly what it means.

Once again, may God bless Donald John Trump.

St. Patrick, pray for us.

APPENDIX 1

Partial List of Pro-Life Accomplishments in President Trump's First Term

(Priests for Life keeps updating this list of President Trump's pro-life accomplishments at ProLifePresident.com)

1. First of all, President Trump did the pro-life movement his greatest service by keeping Hillary Clinton out of the White House. Had she been elected, the extremism of abortion in America would have reached a fever pitch unlike anything we've seen before.

2. President Trump fulfilled his campaign pledge to only appoint pro-life justices to the Supreme Court when he appointed Justice Neil Gorsuch and Justice Brett Kavanaugh. Also, he has placed another 191 conservative judges on the circuit and district courts, bringing significant change even to the liberal ninth circuit.

3. President Trump has deprived the abortion industry of billions of dollars. He signed legislation to permit the states to defund Planned Parenthood of Title X family planning. He also issued an executive order to give states the option to withhold Medicaid and other federal money from organizations that perform abortions, including Planned Parenthood.

4. President Trump implemented the Protect Life Rule, a rule by the Department of Health and Human Services

to cut taxpayer funding under the Title X program for any facility that performs abortions or refers clients to them, such as Planned Parenthood.

5. President Trump reinstated and expanded the "Mexico City Policy." His new policy ensures that our tax dollars are protected from funding the abortion industry overseas across ALL global health spending, not just family planning dollars. The Bush-era Mexico City Policy protected roughly $500 million in spending; the new Trump policy protects over $8.8 billion in overseas aide from funding abortion. He also stopped funding the pro-abortion United Nations Population Fund (UNFPA).

6. The Trump administration Department of Health and Human Services issued a rule requiring that insurers specify to their customers whether the plan they are buying covers abortion. The administration also requested input on how to better enforce the limited abortion provisions contained in Obamacare.

7. The president created a new office in the federal government for Conscience and Religious Freedom so that people who, for example, are being forced to participate in abortion can have their rights vindicated more effectively.

8. President Trump has ended the Obama assault on the religious freedom of those employers who do not want to cover abortion-inducing drugs in the health insurance plans they offer their employees.

9. The president continues to make numerous appointments, across the federal administration, of strong pro-life advocates, starting with Vice-President Mike Pence. Most of the many others he has appointed do not make the

headlines, but they are making and implementing policies and practices that advance the pro-life agenda. For instance, in the Department of Health and Human Services, the strategy memo makes it clear that "human beings" include babies in the womb.

10. The president has pushed hard for the Senate to pass additional pro-life legislation, like the Pain Capable Unborn Child Protection Act, as well as the full removal of funding from Planned Parenthood. He has promised to sign both bills.

APPENDIX 2

General List of Accomplishments in Trump's First Term[1]

- Low-wage workers are benefiting from higher minimum wages and corporations that are increasing entry-level pay.
- Trump signed the biggest wilderness protection and conservation bill in a decade and designated 375,000 acres as protected land.
- Trump signed the Save our Seas Act which funds $10 million per year to clean tons of plastic and garbage from the ocean.
- Trump signed an executive order this year that forces all healthcare providers to disclose the cost of their services so that Americans can comparison shop and know how much less providers charge insurance companies. When signing that bill he said no American should be blindsided by bills for medical services they never agreed to in advance. Hospitals will now be required to post their standard charges for services, which include gross charges, the negotiated rates with insurers and the discounted price a hospital is willing to accept from a patient.

---

[1]   Robby Starbuck, "List of Trump Accomplishments in the Years: 2017, 2018, and 2019," https://www.docdroid.net/KDaSuMo/ trumpaccomplishments.pdf. Starbuck tweets as @robbystarbuck.

- He signed a bill this year allowing some drug imports from Canada so that prescription prices would go down. In the eight years prior to President Trump's inauguration, prescription drug prices increased by an average of 3.6 percent per year. Fast forward to today, and prescription drug prices have seen year-over-year declines in nine of the last ten months, with a 1.1 percent drop as of the most recent month. In June 2019, the United States saw the largest single-year drop (2.0 percent year-over-year decline) in prescription drug prices since 1967.
- Created a White House VA Hotline to help veterans and principally staffed it with veterans and direct family members of veterans. VA employees are being held accountable for poor performance, with more than 4,000 VA employees removed, demoted, and suspended so far.
- Issued an executive order requiring the Secretaries of Defense, Homeland Security, and Veterans Affairs to submit a joint plan to provide veterans access to mental health treatment as they transition to civilian life.
- Because of a bill signed and championed by Trump, in 2020, most federal employees will see their pay increase by an average of 3.1 percent — the largest raise in more than 10 years.
- Trump signed into a law up to 12 weeks of paid parental leave for millions of federal workers. Trump administration will provide HIV prevention drug

for free to 200,000 uninsured patients per year for 11 years.

- All time record sales during the 2019 holidays.
- Trump signed an order allowing small businesses to group together when buying insurance so they can get it at a better price.
- President Trump signed the Preventing Maternal Deaths Act which was written by a Republican lawmaker that provides funding for states to develop maternal mortality review committees to better understand maternal complications and identify solutions and largely focuses on reducing the higher mortality rates for Black Americans.
- In 2018, President Trump signed the groundbreaking First Step Act, a criminal justice bill which enacted reforms that make our justice system fairer and help former inmates successfully return to society. The First Step Act's reforms addressed inequities in sentencing laws that disproportionately harmed Black Americans and reformed mandatory minimums that created unfair outcomes. Over 90 percent of those benefitting from the retroactive sentencing reductions in the First Step Act are Black Americans. The First Step Act expanded judicial discretion in sentencing of non-violent crimes. The First Step Act provides rehabilitative programs to inmates, helping them successfully rejoin society and not return to crime.
- Trump increased funding for Historically Black

Colleges and Universities (HBCUs) by more than 14 percent.

- Trump signed legislation forgiving Hurricane Katrina debt that threatened HBCUs. Made HBCUs a priority by creating the position of executive director of the White House Initiative on HBCUs.
- Trump received the Bipartisan Justice Award at a historically black college for his criminal justice reform accomplishments.
- New single-family home sales are up 31.6 percent in October 2019 compared to just one year ago.
- The poverty rate fell to a 17-year low of 11.8 percent under the Trump administration as a result of a jobs-rich environment.
- Poverty rates for African-Americans and Hispanic-Americans have reached their lowest levels since the U.S. began collecting such data.
- President Trump signed a bill that creates five national monuments, expands several national parks, adds 1.3 million acres of wilderness, and permanently reauthorizes the Land and Water Conservation Fund.
- Trump's USDA committed more than $124 Million to help rebuild rural water infrastructure.
- Consumer confidence and small business confidence at an all time high.
- More than 7 million jobs created since election. More Americans are now employed than ever recorded before in our history. More than 400,000 manufacturing jobs created since his election.

- Trump appointed 5 openly gay ambassadors.
- Trump ordered his openly gay ambassador to Germany, Ric Grenell, to lead a global initiative to decriminalize homosexuality across the globe.
- Through Trump's Anti-Trafficking Coordination Team (ACTeam) initiative, Federal law enforcement more than doubled convictions of human traffickers and increased the number of defendants charged by 75 percent in ACTeam districts.
- In 2018, the Department of Justice (DOJ) dismantled an organization that was the internet's leading source of prostitution-related advertisements resulting in sex trafficking.
- The Office of Management and Budget published new anti-trafficking guidance for government procurement officials to more effectively combat human trafficking. Trump's Immigration and Customs Enforcement's Homeland Security Investigations arrested 1,588 criminals associated with Human Trafficking. United States law enforcement officers are collaborating with Mexican law enforcement officials to dismantle human trafficking networks operating across the U.S.-Mexico border.
- Trump's Department of Health and Human Services provided funding to support the National Human Trafficking Hotline to identify perpetrators and give victims the help they need. That hotline identified 16,862 potential human trafficking cases and provided 14,419 referrals to services between October 2017 and March 2019. Trump's DOJ provided

grants to organizations that support human trafficking victims – serving nearly 9,000 cases from July 1, 2017, to June 30, 2018. The Department of Homeland Security has hired more victim assistance specialists, helping ensure that victims have the proper resources and support.

- President Trump has called on Congress to pass school choice legislation so that no child is trapped in a failing school because of his or her zip code. The President signed funding legislation in September 2018 that increased funding for school choice by $42 million. The tax cuts signed into law by President Trump promote school choice by allowing families to use 529 college savings plans for elementary and secondary education.

- Under his leadership ISIS has lost most of their territory and been largely dismantled. ISIS leader Abu Bakr Al-Baghdadi was killed.

- Signed the first Perkins CTE reauthorization since 2006, authorizing more than $1 billion for states each year to fund vocational and career education programs.

- Executive order expanding apprenticeship opportunities for students and workers.

- President Trump issued an executive order prohibiting the U.S. government from discriminating against Christians or punishing expressions of faith.

- Signed an executive order that allows the government to withhold money from college campuses deemed to be anti-Semitic and who fail to combat anti-Semitism.

- President Trump has ordered a halt to all U.S. taxpayer money going to international organizations that fund or perform abortions.
- Trump imposed sanctions on the socialists in Venezuela who have killed their citizens.
- Finalized new trade agreement with South Korea.
- Made a deal with the European Union to increase U.S. energy exports to Europe.
- Withdrew the U.S. from the job killing TPP deal.
- Secured $250 billion in new trade and investment deals in China and $12 billion in Vietnam.
- OK'd up to $12 billion in aid for farmers affected by unfair trade retaliation.
- Has had over a dozen US hostages freed, including those Obama could not get freed.
- Trump signed the Music Modernization Act, the biggest change to copyright law in decades.
- Trump secured billions that will fund the building of a wall at our southern border.
- The Trump administration is promoting second chance hiring to give former inmates the opportunity to live crime-free lives and find meaningful employment.
- The Department of Education is expanding an initiative that allows individuals in prison to receive Pell Grants to better prepare themselves for the workforce.
- The Department of Justice and Bureau of Prisons

launched a new "Ready to Work Initiative" to help connect employers directly with former prisoners.

- President Trump's historic tax cut legislation included new Opportunity Zone Incentives to promote investment in low-income communities across the country. 8,764 communities across the country have been designated as Opportunity Zones. Opportunity Zones are expected to spur $100 billion in long-term private capital investment in economically distressed communities across the country.
- Trump directed the Education Secretary to end Common Core.
- Trump signed the 9/11 Victims Compensation Fund into law.
- Trump signed measure funding prevention programs for Veteran suicide.
- Companies have brought back over a trillion dollars from overseas because of the TCJA bill that Trump signed.
- Manufacturing jobs growing at the fastest rate in more than 30 years.
- Stock Market has reached record highs.
- Median household income has hit highest level ever recorded.
- African-American unemployment is at an all-time low.
- Hispanic-American unemployment is at an all-time low.
- Asian-American unemployment is at an all-time low.
- Women's unemployment rate is at a 65-year low.

- Youth unemployment is at a 50-year low.
- We have the lowest unemployment rate ever recorded.
- The Pledge to America's Workers has resulted in employers committing to train more than 4 million Americans.
- 95 percent of U.S. manufacturers are optimistic about the future— the highest ever.
- As a result of the Republican tax bill, small businesses will have the lowest top marginal tax rate in more than 80 years.
- Record number of regulations eliminated that hurt small businesses.
- Signed welfare reform requiring able-bodied adults who don't have children to work or look for work if they're on welfare.
- Under Trump, the FDA approved more affordable generic drugs than ever before in history.
- Reformed the Medicare program to stop hospitals from overcharging low-income seniors on their drugs—saving seniors hundreds of millions of dollars this year alone.
- Signed Right-To-Try legislation which allows terminally ill patients to try any experimental treatment that wasn't allowed before.
- Secured $6 billion in new funding to fight the opioid epidemic.
- Signed VA Choice Act and VA Accountability Act, expanded VA telehealth services, walk-in-clinics, and same-day urgent primary and mental health care.

- U.S. oil production recently reached all-time high so we are less dependent on oil from the Middle East.
- The U.S. is a net natural gas exporter for the first time since 1957.
- Withdrew the United States from the job-killing Paris Climate Accord in 2017 and that same year the U.S. still led the world by having the largest reduction in Carbon emissions.
- NATO allies increased their defense spending because of his pressure campaign.
- Created Space Force and got it signed into law as our 6th military branch.
- Has his circuit court judges being confirmed faster than any other new administration.
- Had his Supreme Court Justice's Neil Gorsuch and Brett Kavanaugh confirmed.
- Moved U.S. Embassy in Israel to Jerusalem.
- Agreed to a new trade deal with Mexico & Canada that will increase jobs here and money coming in.
- Reached a breakthrough agreement with the E.U. to increase U.S. exports.
- Imposed tariffs on China in response to China's forced technology transfer, intellectual property theft, and their chronically abusive trade practices.
- Has agreed to a part 1 trade deal with China. (Still negotiating part 2.)
- Signed legislation to improve the National Suicide Hotline.
- Signed the most comprehensive childhood cancer

legislation ever into law, which will advance childhood cancer research and improve treatments.

- Another upcoming accomplishment to add: In
the next week or two Trump will be signing the
first major anti-robocall law in decades called the
TRACED Act (Telephone Robocall Abuse Criminal Enforcement and Deterrence). Once it's law the
TRACED Act will extend the period of time the
FCC has to catch and punish those who intention-
ally break telemarketing restrictions. The bill also
requires voice service providers to develop a framework to verify calls are legitimate before they reach
your phone

- The TRACED Act requires carriers to share tools
and the ability to block spam callers with customers
for free. It also changes the fine imposed on spam
telemarketers from $1,500 to $10,000 PER CALL.
Earlier this year, Trump's FCC fined one robocall
guy $120 million.

- The Tax Cuts and Jobs Act signed into law by Trump
doubled the maximum amount of the child tax credit
available to parents and lifted the income limits so
more people could claim it. It also created a new tax
credit for other dependents.

- In 2018, President Trump signed into law a $2.4 bil-
lion funding increase for the Child Care and Development Fund, providing a total of $8.1 billion to
states to fund child care for low-income families.

- The Child and Dependent Care Tax Credit
(CDCTC) signed into law by Trump provides a tax

credit equal to 20-35 percent of child care expenses, $3,000 per child and $6,000 per family, plus Flexible Spending Accounts (FSAs) allow you to set aside up to $5,000 in pre-tax money to use for child care.

- In 2019, President Donald Trump signed the Autism Collaboration, Accountability, Research, Education and Support Act (CARES) into law which allocates $1.8 billion in funding over the next five years to help people with autism spectrum disorder and to help their families.

- In 2019, President Trump signed into law two funding packages providing nearly $19 million in new funding for Lupus specific research and education programs, as well an additional $41.7 billion in funding for the National Institutes of Health (NIH), the most Lupus funding ever.

ABOUT THE
AUTHORS

Jesse Romero is a long-time Catholic evangelist and a retired veteran of the Los Angeles County Sheriff's department. He holds an undergraduate degree in Liberal Arts from Mount St. Mary's College in Los Angeles and a graduate degree in Catholic Theology from Franciscan University of Steubenville. He speaks frequently around the country and is the popular host of two radio shows. To learn more about Jesse and his mission, visit www.jesseromero.com.

John McCullough is a writer and editor. Over the years he has worked as a teacher, newspaper feature writer, salesman, and magazine editor but his favorite occupations, or vocations rather, are those of husband and father.